Praise for *Learning to Co*

"Collaboration is fast becoming one of the most imp... ship in the twenty-first century. This fact is widely acknowledged and yet educators have few resources to teach students how to systematically pursue collaborative problem-solving. Janet Salmons's book fills this gap with this practical guidebook that can be applied across any discipline. Salmons writes in a clear, logical, and engaging style that is research based and creates a sense of excitement and motivation for the collaborative experience."—***Louise Kelly***, *Professor of Management and Leadership, University of La Verne, and Author,* The Psychologist Manager

"Employers keep saying that they want employees who can be good team players and work collaboratively, and Janet Salmons has finally provided faculty and course-writing teams with a useful, well-grounded, and practical guidebook for creating learning experiences that help our students build those critical skill sets. This book will help create truly collaborative learning experiences for our students—and help students move from 'Ugh, group work,' to 'Yes, collaborative teamwork!'"—***William C. Schulz III***, *Director of Academic Initiatives, Office of Academic Affairs, School of Management, and Founding Director, Walden Center for Social Change, Walden University*

"The future of work requires team adaptability, shared participation, and integrated contributions among professionals. Educators need to create thoughtful learning experiences that expose students to relevant, collaboration opportunities they will encounter in a connected world. Janet Salmons's book offers the fundamentals for collaborative learning paired with the pedagogical planning and assessment practices to reach this goal. With reflective questions, team-based design graphs, and visual mapping of the collaborative learning taxonomy, instructors and learning designers will find this book to be a valuable resource for developing guided facilitation for learners." —***Laura Pasquini***, *Senior Lecturer, University of North Texas, and Researcher, The Digital Learning and Social Media Research Group*

"Collaborative learning has an amazing potential for supporting students to learn within a discipline and to grow their agency and capacity for collaborative action. Unfortunately, the literature of learning in groups is also replete with stories of how it all went wrong. This new book by Janet Salmons provides the latest version of her highly accessible and research-based conceptual and visual taxonomy of collaboration and shows us how to apply this rich vocabulary to the design of face-to-face and online collaborative learning that can yield the desired learning benefits while minimizing the pitfalls. And as a bonus the same principles can also be applied to planning successful collaborative research and work processes."—**Tony Carr**, *Convener, elmerge Africa, and Educational Technologist in the Centre for Innovation in Learning and Teaching (CILT), University of Cape Town (South Africa)*

"Collaboration is a part of our life. In this book Janet Salmons illuminates how collaboration can be a positive experience and how we can intentionally learn to be an effective collaborator no matter the circumstances, our role, our preference for way of working, and end point. At a time when working effectively with others is seen as a vital skill, this book unpacks how it is possible to thrive and flourish as we learn to understand the collaborative process, how working with others can be put into practice, and, most importantly, how we can grow as individuals personally and professionally." —**Narelle Lemon**, *Associate Professor, Education, Swinburne University of Technology (Melbourne, Australia)*

"Western understanding of collaborative learning and work in Asia is in stark contrast to the way it is actually practiced among Chinese students. Surprisingly, they do not relish many of our best attempts to design collaborative learning processes. This is due in large part to social loafing, overreliance on linguistic skills of others, crosscultural disconnects, and misalignments in student/teacher expectations. *Learning to Collaborate, Collaborating to Learn* gives instructors a tangible framework to understand, organize, assess, implement, and redesign methodologies toward effective student-centered existential collaborative processes inside or outside the classroom. In our Fieldwork in Leadership Studies course, we strive to give theory practical application. The taxonomical approaches, the assessments, and the activities offered here are invaluable and can give us tangible guidelines to help us improve our deliverables."—**Brendon C. Fox**, *Assistant Professor of Leadership Studies, Fort Hays State University (United States); Sino Partnership with Sias International University (Xinzheng, Henan, China)*

LEARNING TO COLLABORATE, COLLABORATING TO LEARN

LEARNING TO COLLABORATE, COLLABORATING TO LEARN

Engaging Students in the Classroom and Online

Janet Salmons

Foreword by Lynn A. Wilson

Stylus

STERLING, VIRGINIA

Published by Stylus Publishing, LLC.
22883 Quicksilver Drive
Sterling, Virginia 20166-2019

Library of Congress Cataloging-in-Publication Data
Names: Salmons, Janet, 1952- author.
Title: Learning to collaborate, collaborating to learn : engaging students in the classroom and online / Janet Salmons ; foreword by Lynn Wilson.
Description: First edition. | Sterling, Virginia : Stylus Publishing, LLC., 2019. | Includes bibliographical references and index.
Identifiers: LCCN 2018026711| ISBN 9781620368053 (paperback : acid-free paper) | ISBN 9781620368046 (cloth : alk. paper) | ISBN 9781620368060 ((library networkable e-edition) | ISBN 9781620368077 (consumer e-edition)
Subjects: LCSH: Group work in education | Student participation in curriculum planning. | Blended learning. | Flipped classrooms. | Computer-assisted instruction.
Classification: LCC LB1032 .S24 2019 | DDC 371.39/5--dc23
LC record available at https://lccn.loc.gov/2018026711

13-digit ISBN: 978-1-62036-804-6 (cloth)
13-digit ISBN: 978-1-62036-805-3 (paperback)
13-digit ISBN: 978-1-62036-806-0 (library networkable e-edition)
13-digit ISBN: 978-1-62036-807-7 (consumer e-edition)

Printed in the United States of America

All first editions printed on acid-free paper that meets the American National Standards Institute Z39-48 Standard.

First Edition, 2019

To my truly collaborative partner, Cole, thanks always for your love and support (not to mention extra cooking and cleaning while I wrote this book!)

To Panaena, Naomi, Tom, Hannah, Zac, Sammy, Alex, and Oliver, collaborating on our life journeys brings me the greatest joy

CONTENTS

TABLES AND FIGURES

TABLES

FIGURES

The Taxonomy of Collaboration

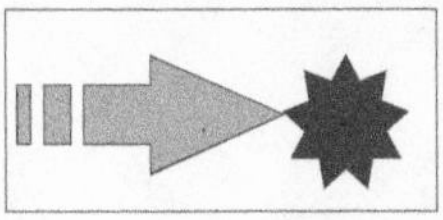	**REFLECTION** Individuals align their own knowledge, attitudes, and skills with group efforts. Individuals make sense of and prepare for their roles in collaborative efforts.
	**DIALOGUE** Participants in the collaborative process agree on and work with the group's communication expectations, time lines, processes, and tools. They exchange ideas to find shared purpose and coherence with the plans and/or tactics needed to coordinate their efforts.
	**REVIEW** Participants exchange work for constructive mutual critique and to incorporate others' perspectives. Participants evaluate which elements of each partner's work should be included in the deliverables, and how they will be integrated into the whole.
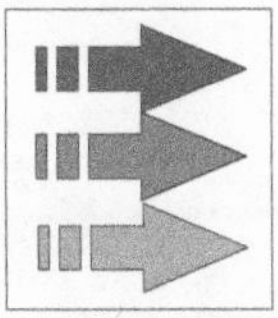	**PARALLEL COLLABORATION** Participants work to each complete a component of the project. Elements are combined into a collective final product, or the process moves to another level of collaboration.
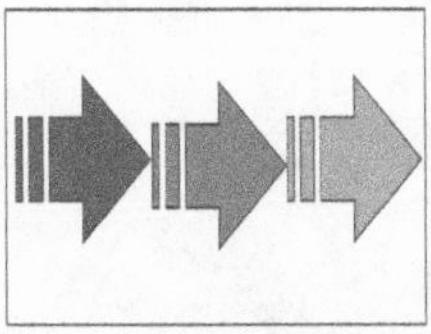	**SEQUENTIAL COLLABORATION** Participants complete stages of the work, building on each other's contributions through a series of progressive steps. All are combined into a collective final product, or the process moves to another level of collaboration.
	**SYNERGISTIC COLLABORATION** Participants synthesize their ideas to plan, organize, and complete the creation of a product that melds all contributions into a collective final product.

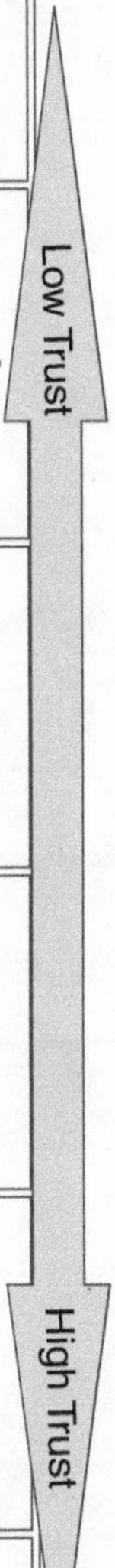

FOREWORD

When asked to write about this book, I immediately reflected on the importance of purposeful collaboration in my work as executive director and chief executive officer of the research and educational global nongovernmental organization SeaTrust Institute, as well as in my own professional academic endeavors. Janet Salmons and I have been collaborating since the day we met as doctoral students, constructing a joint seminar for our peers. She came from the world of education and I from public policy, so from the beginning we were purposefully interdisciplinary in our collaboration. As our careers progressed, we published together; gave joint webinars and trainings; and continued blending our knowledge, methods, and processes to create something that neither of us would have produced alone. We cocreated something we call the Collaboration Integration Paradigm, which found its way into my presentations and trainings for nonprofit and environmental policy practitioners and into my formal presentations as head of delegation for SeaTrust Institute at the United Nations Framework Convention on Climate Change.

As we have continued to refine and apply collaboration principles and tools in our respective academic disciplines as doctoral mentors and faculty, and in our own practitioner roles in public policy and community engagement, Janet took the path of developing scholarship and tools for educators to use in building a personal and social presence for themselves and their students, particularly in the e-learning environment. Collaboration was always central to her projects, which deepened my respect for her processes and contributions; she took her efforts beyond checklists and ventured into the true art and science of collaboration. Rooted in scholarship and applied methodology, Janet always insisted on delivering practical applications from theory, and she continues that tradition in this book. In applying the principles and practical guidance that you will find within this volume, I have put into practice the results of our shared interests and beliefs in interdisciplinary learning for meaningful action. Purposeful, knowledge-informed collaboration makes a difference; it creates shared experiences and enhances outcomes whether applied at the level of global negotiations or in small groups.

The call to collaborate is everywhere you look. Whether you or your students see it as a difficult but necessary element or embrace collaboration as an advanced way to solve problems, it is central to almost any professional endeavor. We have all been in good collaborations and in some that left us wondering why we made the effort. In this book, Janet demonstrates why some collaborations work and why some do not. She provides step-by-step guidance on how we can help others learn to collaborate in ways that enhance their ability to contribute, make a difference, and do not waste others' valuable time. A special gift contained in this book is that, in placing these practical aids firmly within the interdisciplinary traditions and frameworks that show us why they work, this book invites readers to customize their own collaboration designs by incorporating their disciplinary traditions and methods into the process.

The narrative and visual maps will help educators who will use this book in class settings see and experience the different degrees and types of collaboration, build a plan for the type of collaboration that is appropriate for the task, and develop skills to engage in the best collaborative approaches for a specific purpose. Technical, disciplinary, and process skills are needed. Collaborative partners must obtain factual knowledge on the topic to participate. Then they rely on procedural knowledge for group decision-making and collaborative leadership. Self-knowledge is also important because collaborative partners need to recognize their own abilities and limits when it comes to how they work with others. In this book, Janet shows how to guide students or adult learners to best participate in different types of collaborative settings and how to assume different roles. She also provides direction about how to assess a collaboration to see if it achieved what it was designed to do.

But this book is not just for educators. It is for anyone who collaborates, formally or informally, virtually or face-to-face, as group leader or group member. It is not only for those who design or deliver educational products or classroom instruction; it is for anyone in any place where people are learning. Janet's collaborative premise of trust (especially generous trust) delves into the differences in trust at a personal level, a strategic level, and an organizational level. She unpacks the concept of milieu and shows how milieu can enhance or inhibit a collaboration. As she explains the technical and theoretical concepts like social constructivism, you will see how not only your views and perceptions but those of everyone with whom you interact affect the collaborative potential and outcome of your efforts. In learning to recognize your own collaborative style, you will identify your strengths so that you can capitalize on them and accommodate your weaker areas through purposeful collaboration design or by learning new skills.

Whether you are new to collaboration or a seasoned group leader and educator, you will benefit from reading and using this book. As you reflect on the principles of learning to collaborate and collaborating to learn, relax and enjoy knowing that you are in the hands of a knowledgeable and seasoned educator who approaches collaboration with compassion for the people and for the social outcomes that good collaboration can produce. In helping us all better integrate these principles into the legacies we leave, Janet continues to help promote positive social change as an educator through purposeful, knowledge-informed collaboration. I have found great benefit in her approach. I believe you will, too.

Lynn A. Wilson
Port Townsend, Washington, USA
2018

PREFACE

Where did the idea for the *taxonomy of collaboration* originate? The taxonomy and related materials are truly the fruit of scholar-practitioner efforts.

Much of my professional career has involved collaborations of some kind, including both intra- and interorganizational collaboration. In most cases, collaboration, in my experience, has involved working across organizational and disciplinary boundaries. When we add in cross-cultural factors (however we define *culture*), differences in how people see the world through their disciplinary lenses, varied styles of communication, and the use of technology, collaboration is anything but straightforward. Figure P.1 illustrates the intersections that occur when crossing boundaries and cultures.

In an "aha!" moment, I realized that while professional life typically depends on our ability to work together, our educational experiences are typically completed independently. Most often those educational experiences are evaluated on our own performance, whether others were involved or not. I was curious about ways that collaborative learning could go beyond simply offering us the chance to learn the subject matter of the course to including intentional opportunities to better understand the collaborative process and ways it can be put into practice.

Figure P.1. People collaborate within and across disciplines.

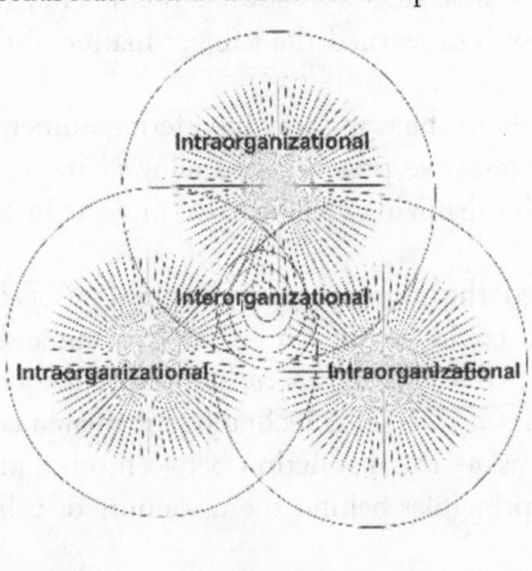

I created the first iteration of a collaboration taxonomy when I was trying to visually communicate types of collaborative work for a conference presentation. That first iteration included the three work designs present in the current model. The next iteration included dialogue, review, and the trust continuum. I used that version as the basis for a qualitative study I conducted from 2004 to 2006 as part of my dissertation research. I interviewed instructors from five countries about how they planned and facilitated collaborative activities and what they had learned from doing so. I inquired whether any aspect of the collaborative process was missing from the taxonomy. Based on their responses, I added the individual component and the focus on ways individuals' reflection and sense-making relates to the accomplishment of shared goals (see Figure 1.3.).

I had the opportunity to design and teach two different academic courses modeled on the taxonomy. Teaching adult students who were themselves in the workforce allowed me to understand more deeply the ways the elements of the taxonomy fit together, as well as the critical factors that allow students to succeed. I conducted another study that involved interviews with alumni who had taken a course that required ongoing collaboration throughout the term and creation of a substantial project with fellow learners. These interviews were most illuminating, and notes from my transcripts have informed comments made in this book about the student experience. The most pertinent and memorable student comments related to their disposition to oppose group assignments prior to taking this class. They uniformly feared an unbalanced work group in which they did more than their share of work and others were able to skate by without doing their part. After taking the class, with clear agreements and fair individual and group assessments, they no longer felt vulnerable to these issues. Certainly, it is not that these all-too-human characteristics had gone away, but that the students now knew a variety of strategies to address them. They had indeed learned to collaborate, as well as learned the subject matter of the course through collaborative methods.

I also learned about the taxonomy by offering numerous workshops and webinars. These interactive presentations allowed me to hear from people who struggled with organizing collaborative projects in the classroom or in professional life.

When I started the journey of developing this taxonomy, I focused on the ways that it could be used in online learning and virtual collaborations. I variously titled it *taxonomy of collaborative e-learning* and *taxonomy of online collaboration*. Over time, as technology-mediated communication has become more pervasive, the distinction between on- and offline seems less pronounced. The principles behind the taxonomy of collaboration focused on the people who were working together, and they apply whether we interact electronically some or all of the time.

I hope you will find that this framework, and this book, which is dedicated to explaining and applying it, will be helpful as you organize collaborative projects in and out of the classroom. I welcome the opportunity to hear about your experiences and hope you will contact me to share your examples or to ask any questions.

PART ONE

THINKING ABOUT COLLABORATION

I

COLLABORATION IN A CONNECTED WORLD

The illiterate of the future will not be the person who cannot read. It will be the person who does not know how to learn.

—Alvin Toffler, 1970

Objectives

Chapter 1 will prepare you to:

- Understand the premises and terminology used throughout this book.
- Explain reasons for choosing to teach with collaborative methods.
- Describe the basic principles associated with Bloom's taxonomies, the knowledge learning model, and the taxonomy of online collaboration.

Introduction

What does *learning to collaborate, collaborating to learn* mean? This system of thinking is based on four premises. (Chapter 2 explores the theoretical underpinnings for these premises.) One premise is that collaboration is the synthesis of multiple processes that involve both individual and group efforts. While collaboration is widely discussed, existing resources often refer to it in a simplistic way and make overly broad distinctions between collaborative and individual work. "Learning to collaborate, collaborating to learn" approaches recognize the role of individual reflection and sense-making as essential to collaboration in an educational context. A second premise is that there are many types and degrees of collaboration. Collaborative partners need to agree about what they intend to produce together and the most appropriate approach to use to address the problem or complete the assignment. A third premise is that successful collaboration requires thoughtful plans, communication and conflict resolution, work arrangements and management. The fourth premise is that when some or all of these interactions occur online, collaborative partners need to agree on the technologies and strategies they will use when they work synchronously or asynchronously. Finally specific knowledge, skills, and abilities associated with these premises can be learned when assignments, learning goals, and assessments are designed to address them. Hibbert and Huxham (2005) described what collaborators need to learn to be effective:

> Learning [is] associated with understanding how to make judgments about, and seek to manage, trust, power, goals and opportunism in collaborative contexts [and] learning associated with understanding how to effect mutual communication, engage with partners' procedures, negotiate politics and develop effective structures and processes for the particular collaboration. (p. 66)

Some of us are predisposed to working with others and find collaboration comes naturally, while others are more comfortable getting things done on their own. We will probably find ourselves in situations with both kinds of people. Sometimes it is simple to sit down with our partners and come to an agreement about how to proceed; other times our partners are located across the globe or have very different cultural or educational backgrounds. Based on these and other characteristics of contemporary collaboration, it is important to learn how to collaborate with diverse collaborative partners who may or may not be physically present. In a connected world, collaboration can span boundaries of geography, time, culture, sector, or organization, as well as discipline.

It would seem that today's students should be prepared to use technology to communicate and collaborate because online communication for social purposes has become pervasive. Whether using a computer on a desk or a mobile device on the go, most people are electronically connected. But do they know how to leverage such connections to produce unique and valuable results? Can they translate the skills used for casual exchange into skills needed for working on a virtual team or leading a complex cross-cultural collaboration? Can they communicate and organize projects with others whose knowledge basis, worldviews, agendas, ways of thinking, and decision-making are entirely unfamiliar? If we are collaborating electronically, we need to know preferences, such as using attachments versus posting in a shared drive or timing for response to e-mailed questions.

Students acquire these competencies in order to achieve the potential advantages that can be gained from meshing individual work with others' contributions. They can do so through learning activities, assignments, and projects that are designed and facilitated with this goal in mind. At the same time, social learning and social constructivist thinkers have long argued that we can learn from and with each other. "Learning to collaborate, collaborating to learn" means we plan and teach in ways that accomplish both goals: Students gain the competencies they will need to collaborate with others while at the same time acquiring subject matter knowledge. We account for the role of individual efforts to prepare and reflect; we state and use measurable criteria by which we can assess the success of the collaborative effort as a whole and the input of each collaborative partner.

What Is Collaboration, and Why Is It Important?

The word *collaborate* has its origins in the Latin word *collaborare*, "to work together" with a purpose: "the action of working with someone to produce something" (Soanes & Stevenson, 2004 p. 280). While the terms *teamwork* and *collaboration* are closely related, they are not precisely synonymous. Teams may rely on collaborative—or individual—efforts to accomplish shared goals. Collaborative partners work toward accomplishing shared goals with a specific process. Collaboration is a process that involves meshing ideas, approaches, and contributions into a uniquely representative outcome. While participants may complete parts of a project independently, when they integrate their efforts into one outcome, we can describe their work as collaboration. When people collaborate, they think together as well as work together. As collaborative partners they can acquire new insights on the subject matter, build skills, generate innovative ideas, or develop new applications for best practices. For the purpose of this book, *collaboration* is defined as an interactive process that engages two or more participants who work together to achieve outcomes they could not accomplish independently.

When assignments are designed for completion by collaborative partners, the objective is for peers to learn from and with each other. This instructional approach is called *collaborative learning* and is defined for the purpose of this book as constructing knowledge, negotiating meanings, and/or solving problems through mutual engagement of two or more learners in a coordinated effort.

This definition of collaborative learning draws on the constructivist and social constructivist theories that suggest learning is the construction of knowledge. (Theoretical foundations are discussed in detail in chapter 2.) "Constructing knowledge, negotiating meanings, and/or solving problems" refers to a process of learning together in meaningful ways that use and develop higher order thinking skills. "Two or more learners" means that activities engage pairs or groups of students. Others, including the instructor or people outside the class, may also be a part of the collaborative learning activity. "Coordinated effort" means that the project is purposeful and meshes with learning goals.

In online or hybrid classes, interaction between learners and instructors occurs electronically. Online learners interact through discussions and activities involving the whole class, small groups, or dyads. *Collaborative e-learning* is defined for the purpose of this book as follows: Constructing knowledge, negotiating meanings, and/or solving problems through mutual engagement of two or more learners in a coordinated effort, using information and communication technologies (ICTs) for some or all of the interactions.

While some in the field use the terms *cooperative learning* and *collaborative learning* interchangeably, there is a significant distinction between collaborative and cooperative learning. Teaseley and Roschelle (1995) differentiated between the terms as follows:

> Cooperative work is accomplished through the division of labor among participants, where each person is responsible for a portion of the problem solving, whereas collaboration involves the mutual engagement of participants in a coordinated effort to solve the problem together. (p. 70)

Collaborative learning emphasizes learner–learner interaction in situations where the learners have some level of autonomy or responsibility for determining how decisions are made for accomplishing the learning goal. McInnerney and Roberts (2004) point to the educator's roles in organizing the tasks and roles in the group, since, in the cooperative learning model, the teacher retains control and, in the collaborative learning model, the teacher relinquishes more control to the learners. The term *cooperative learning* should be used when students are required to work in small groups formed and guided by the instructor. The term *collaborative learning* should be used when students are responsible for determining their own approaches to taking roles and agreeing to the process they will use to organize, coordinate, and complete learning tasks. Collaborative learning encourages students to learn *how* to collaborate.

The Collaborative Knowledge Learning Model

With whom do students collaborate? Do inexperienced students learn from experienced students, or do they work together to study new topics none of them previously understood? Do they collaborate to develop ways to address dilemmas or solve problems? The ways we design and plan assignments vary greatly depending on the answers we give to these kinds of questions. The collaborative knowledge learning model (Table 1.1) helps us to be more precise by differentiating among the following four broad types of collaborative learning:

1. *Knowledge cocreation* refers to collaborative generation of new knowledge, solutions, or practices.
2. *Knowledge acquisition* describes learning that takes place when people come together to acquire new skills or knowledge that none of the participants had prior to the collaboration.
3. *Knowledge transfer* describes ways we learn from a partner by sharing our expertise or knowledge.
4. *Knowledge exchange* describes learning that occurs when we share information and resources with another person.

For example, let's say we are trying to fulfill an assignment to write an essay collaboratively. You might give me tips on formatting in American Psychological Association (APA) style, and I might give you some relevant articles. We are exchanging knowledge and resources. Even at this basic level, skills and agreements smooth the way. You need to know that the requirement for error-free APA will present a challenge for me. I need to know what articles you would find useful.

If you know how to write an essay and I don't, you could show me the approaches you've used and thereby transfer your knowledge to me. The instructor may have paired us for the purpose of having a less experienced student work with a more experienced peer. The instructor might also use this approach to make strategic use of other professionals or paraprofessionals such as teaching assistants or writing program instructors. If we both

TABLE 1.1
Collaborative Knowledge Learning Model

Type of Learning	*Description*
Knowledge Cocreation	Learning activities that invite students to collaboratively generate original ideas or solutions
Knowledge Acquisition	Learning activities that invite students to collaboratively develop new skills or competencies
Knowledge Transfer	Learning activities that invite students to learn from another person who has more knowledge
Knowledge Exchange	Learning activities that invite students to mutually share ideas or resources

have prior experience with writing essays, we can transfer on a mutual basis, teach each other, and learn each other's strategies. If neither of us knows how to write an essay, we can acquire techniques and learn together. If the essay assignment asks us to solve a problem, interpret a case, or discover a new angle on course content, we can work together to cocreate a new approach.

In other words, when we need information or resources, we collaborate to exchange and share. When one knows something the other does not, one learns from the other through knowledge transfer. When both need new knowledge, they collaborate to acquire new knowledge together. When the collaborative partners think together and create their own new ideas, they are cocreating knowledge. As educators we may organize the learning experiences to promote one or more of these styles of learning. The way we do so will depend on our assessment of a variety of factors: curricular goals and subject matter; time available to complete the assignment; and characteristics, experience, and academic level of the students. The approach may also depend on the degree of collaboration we hope students will achieve. Do we hope for them to simply share—or to mesh—ideas, concepts, practices, or methodologies? What collaboration competencies and what subject matter mastery will the learning experience develop? Given these questions and implications for facilitation and assessment, what do educators need to know to create worthwhile collaborative learning experiences? The taxonomy of collaboration is designed for this purpose.

Taxonomies as Conceptual Frameworks

The taxonomy of collaboration builds on the work of Benjamin Bloom and others who have developed taxonomies for educational purposes. What is an educational taxonomy? Scientists have used the term *taxonomy* to describe biological systems. Gilbert (1992) described a taxonomy as a system of categories or classifications that are used for purposes of organization, conceptualization, and communication. Bloom interpreted the concept of the taxonomy for educational purposes. He observed that, beyond just classifying observations, a taxonomy should clarify the relationships among classes of phenomena. "While a classification scheme may have many arbitrary elements . . . a taxonomy must be so constructed that the order of the terms must correspond to some 'real' order among the phenomena represented by the terms" (Bloom, Engelhart, Furst, Hill, & Krathwohl, 1956, p. 17). The system used in Bloom's taxonomies is ordered from simple to complex based on the assumption that objectives from one level are likely to make use of and be built on the behaviors found in the preceding level (Bloom et al., 1956).

The Bloom team aimed to classify "intended behaviors of students—the ways in which individuals are to act, think or feel as a result of participating in some unit of instruction" (Bloom et al., 1956, p. 12). They did not intend to classify instructional methods or styles. Their guiding principle was neutrality, to the extent possible. They compared their work to the Dewey decimal system in a library, which classifies books but does not represent a judgment of their value or quality. Several key points are important in regard to the purpose Bloom and colleagues (1956) hoped to achieve. One is the need for specificity of learning objectives, and a second is the need for congruence among objectives, learning activities, and evaluation. A third is that the taxonomy would provide a common language for communication among educators who often work in the isolation of the classroom.

Materials known as Bloom's taxonomy are actually the product of a team of five researchers: Max Engelhart, Edward Furst, Walker Hill, David Krathwohl, and Benjamin Bloom (Bloom et al., 1956). Acknowledging the many ways people learn, they identified three domains: cognitive, affective, and psychomotor. While these are three distinct taxonomies, Bloom and the team recognized that important relationships exist between cognitive and affective domains. The *cognitive domain* encompasses both critical and creative thinking. The *affective domain* describes ways that learners' attitudes, motivation, participation, and ultimate change result from the interrelated development in cognitive and affective domains.

The *taxonomy of educational objectives* for the cognitive domain is a framework that shows six levels of thinking, from knowledge through evaluation. It focuses on the development of critical thinking skills, beginning with the ability to retain terminology and basic concepts of a subject and moving toward the ability to use them in other contexts, improve upon the concepts through synthesis, and ultimately critically evaluate concepts or phenomena (Bloom et al., 1956). The taxonomy derived much of its philosophical foundation from the work of John Dewey. Bloom echoes Dewey's view that educators must expect more than rote learning. Both Dewey and Bloom believed that "knowledge is of little value if it cannot be utilized in new situations or in a form very different from that in which it was originally encountered" (Bloom et al., 1956, p. 29). (See chapter 2 for more on theoretical foundations.)

Forty-five years after Bloom's team put together the taxonomies, a group of people went through a similar process of meetings and discussions in an effort to update the cognitive domain. Lorin Anderson, a former student of Bloom's, and one of the original team members, David Krathwohl, led the revision team. The team was made up of experts from the fields of cognitive psychology, curriculum theory, and testing and assessment. The result of their work was published as *Taxonomy for Learning, Teaching and Assessing: A Revision of Bloom's Taxonomy of Educational Objectives* (Anderson, Bloom, Krathwohl, & Airasian, 2000). Differentiations between the original and revised taxonomies include both sequence and content. The names of the six major categories were changed from *noun* to *verb* forms to reflect a greater priority on learning as an active process (Krathwohl, 2002) (see Table 1.2). The knowledge category in the original version was explained as follows: "The student can give evidence that he remembers, either by recalling or by recognizing, some idea or phenomenon" (Bloom et al., 1956, p. 28).

The revision differentiates aspects of the knowledge dimension to include factual knowledge, conceptual knowledge, procedural knowledge, and metacognitive knowledge (Anderson et al., 2000). The knowledge dimension intersects with cognitive processes in this two-dimensional representation. The update to the original taxonomy allows for more fine-grained distinctions between, for example, the kind of learning that occurs when we ask students to analyze facts versus concepts or procedures (see Table 1.3.).

The updated taxonomy of educational objectives for the affective domain is a framework that shows six levels of development in attitudes and values (Krathwohl, Bloom, & Masia, 1964). At the most basic level is the ability to receive experiences or information. Affective domain categories explain how the process of learning builds from having initial willingness to receive new ideas to having the motivation to respond and engage with others. In the next levels, the individual attaches value to the phenomenon or behavior, prioritizes, and organizes ways to respond. Students are able to bring together values (and possible disparate values), resolve conflicts between them, and begin to build an internally consistent value system (Bloom, Krathwohl, & Masia, 1964; Gronlund, 2003). At level 5, behaviors are consistent with internalized values.

TABLE 1.2
The Cognitive Domain in the 1956 and 2000 Versions

Original Bloom's Taxonomy	*Revised Bloom's Taxonomy*
Evaluation	Create
Synthesis	Evaluate
Analysis	Analyze
Application	Apply
Comprehension	Understand
Knowledge	Remember

TABLE 1.3

The Updated Taxonomy for Learning, Teaching, and Assessing

Cognitive Process Dimension					
Remember Retrieve relevant knowledge from long-term memory.	**Understand** Construct meaning from instructional messages.	**Apply** Carry out or use the procedure in a given situation.	**Analyze** Break material into its constituent parts and determine how the parts relate to one another in an overall structure or purpose.	**Evaluate** Make judgments based on criteria and standards.	**Create** Put elements together to form a coherent or functional whole; recognize elements in a new pattern or structure.

The Knowledge Dimension intersects with each cognitive process depending on the type:

A. **Factual Knowledge:** The basic elements. Students must know to be acquainted with the discipline or solve problems in it.

B. **Conceptual Knowledge:** The interrelationships among the basic elements within the larger structure that enable them to function together.

C. **Procedural Knowledge:** How to do something, methods of inquiry, and criteria for using them.

D. **Metacognitive Knowledge:** Knowledge of cognition in general as well as awareness and knowledge of one's own cognition.

(Adapted from Anderson, Bloom, Krathwohl, & Airasian, 2000)

The original and updated versions of Bloom's taxonomy for the cognitive domain show relationships between basic and advanced learning. By incorporating the affective domain as well, educators invite students to connect with their own motivations for learning and commit to ethical standards. These taxonomies are useful for those who plan and design educational offerings because they provide organizational frameworks for scaffolding increasingly complex assignments. Instead of finding Bloom's taxonomies overly prescriptive, educators have reimagined them in ways that fit their pedagogical and curricular contexts. However, these taxonomies have their limitations—namely, they are focused primarily on the efforts of individual students in traditional classroom settings. The taxonomy of collaboration introduces ways to think about social learning in an era when students are accustomed to communicating by means of various kinds of electronic technologies.

Introduction to the Taxonomy of Collaboration

The taxonomy of collaboration has three main components: collaborative processes, levels of collaboration, and the trust continuum (see Figure 1.1). The three processes are common to any collaboration: individual reflection, dialogue, and mutual critique through review. Three distinct levels offer increasingly complex ways that tasks, roles, and outcomes can be organized by collaborative partners, with guidance from the instructor or leader. The trust continuum reminds us that from the simplest to most highly integrated level, the development of trust among collaborative partners and commitment to the collaborative process is essential.

While presented in a linear fashion, in practice the taxonomy is flexible and recursive. Processes and levels can be combined in various ways to create multicourse curricula, multistage course projects, or multistep assignments. Circumstances that might affect choice of collaborative processes and level(s) include the nature of the task, assignment purpose and goals, participant characteristics, project time frame, and desired outcomes.

The taxonomy illustrates elements of collaboration, regardless of the place they occur or the means of communication used. However, it offers particular ways to think through each element in the context of collaborative processes that include technology-mediated interactions. Circumstances that might affect choice of *online* collaborative style include participants' experience with ICTs, level of existing relationship and trust among members, experience using leadership, decision-making, and project coordination skills online.

Figure 1.1. The taxonomy of collaboration.

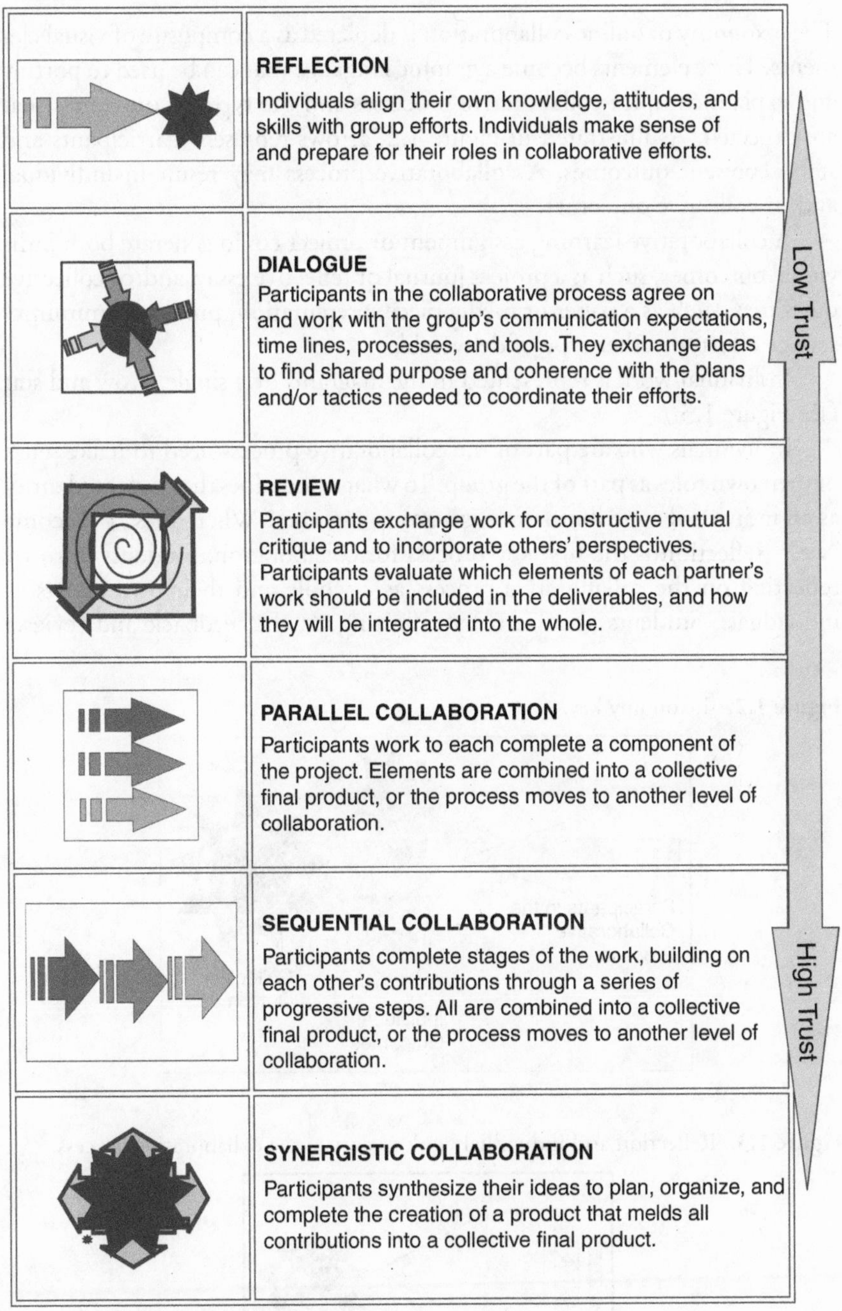
REFLECTION
Individuals align their own knowledge, attitudes, and skills with group efforts. Individuals make sense of and prepare for their roles in collaborative efforts.
DIALOGUE
Participants in the collaborative process agree on and work with the group's communication expectations, time lines, processes, and tools. They exchange ideas to find shared purpose and coherence with the plans and/or tactics needed to coordinate their efforts.
REVIEW
Participants exchange work for constructive mutual critique and to incorporate others' perspectives. Participants evaluate which elements of each partner's work should be included in the deliverables, and how they will be integrated into the whole.
PARALLEL COLLABORATION
Participants work to each complete a component of the project. Elements are combined into a collective final product, or the process moves to another level of collaboration.
SEQUENTIAL COLLABORATION
Participants complete stages of the work, building on each other's contributions through a series of progressive steps. All are combined into a collective final product, or the process moves to another level of collaboration.
SYNERGISTIC COLLABORATION
Participants synthesize their ideas to plan, organize, and complete the creation of a product that melds all contributions into a collective final product.
Low Trust
High Trust

Elements of the Taxonomy of Online Collaboration

The taxonomy of online collaboration is depicted as a composite of visual elements. These elements become a graphic language that can be used to portray and explain complex collaborative processes and the types of outcomes that are expected. As illustrated in Figure 1.2, arrows represent participants and stars represent outcomes. A collaborative process may result in individual and/or collective outcomes.

A collaborative learning assignment or project could generate both individual outcomes, such as a project journal or reflective essay, and/or collective outcomes, such as a paper or media piece, presentation, project, community service effort, or other type of deliverable.

Individual work is represented in the diagrams by a single arrow and star (see Figure 1.3.).

Individuals who are part of the collaborative process need to make sense of their own roles as part of the group. To what extent does the student identify as an individual contributor versus a group member? When does "I" become "we"? Reflection is the first key process for collaboration. Students learn by reflecting on the collaborative process as a whole and their own efforts as individuals. Students also learn by reflecting on the feedback and reviews

Figure 1.2. Taxonomy key.

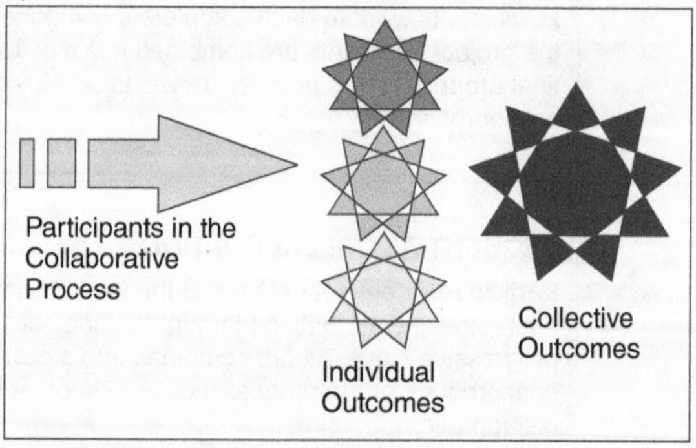

Figure 1.3. Reflection and individual work as part of the collaborative process.

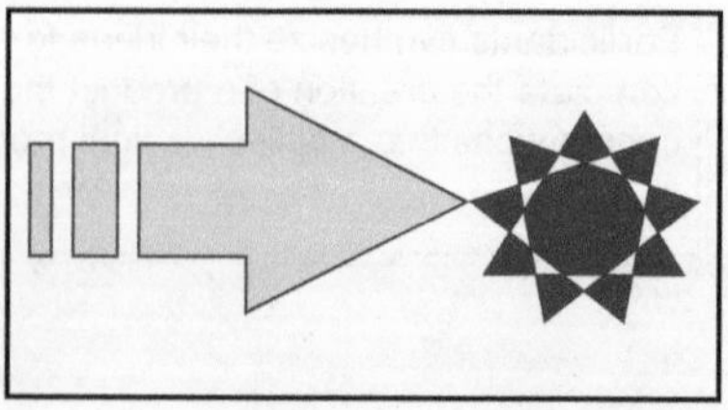

they receive from collaborative partners, other students, the instructor, and any external players. Self-awareness and knowledge of one's own cognition is enhanced through reflection, meaning students can be better prepared to exchange or transfer, acquire, or cocreate knowledge with their partners. Through these experiences, students have the opportunity to grow in the affective domain when they develop, understand, share, and apply their own values to the collaborative effort. Reflection is inherent in the efforts students make to internalize their own value systems.

The individual reflection element of the taxonomy of collaboration also aligns with the Bloom's taxonomy cognitive domain. Students construct their own meanings for the learning that occurs, in addition to the meanings constructed together with collaborative partners. Individuals are responsible for evaluating the evolution of the group's relationships, agreements, and the work they produce.

Reflective activities could include journaling, blogging, or creating a portfolio. From instructional and assessment standpoints, individual learning activities can generate additional deliverables that help instructors monitor individual participation and performance. (See chapter 6 for more about designing and planning reflective learning activities. See chapter 7 for more about assessing individual work.)

Individuals need to communicate in order to collaborate; thus, dialogue is the second key process of collaboration. Dialogue is both the foundational level of collaboration and the glue that holds it together throughout all stages. As defined here, *dialogue* refers to a focused interaction. Dialogue, as part of the collaborative process, challenges participants to find coherence in diverse ideas, plans, and tactics needed to coordinate their efforts. Students discuss the ways they intend to exchange, transfer, acquire, or cocreate knowledge as

Figure 1.4. Dialogue.

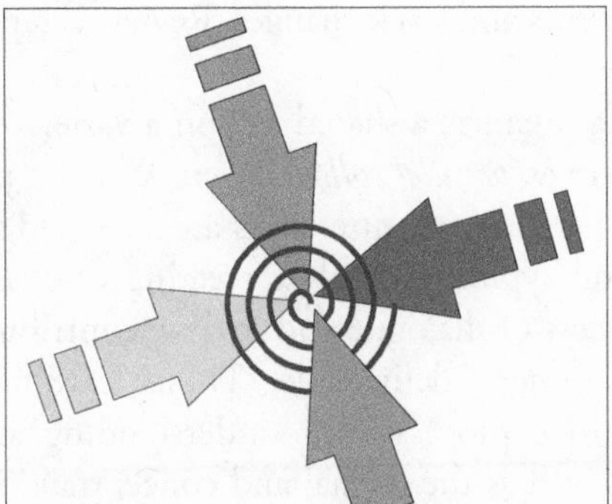

needed to succeed with the assignment. Dialogue is represented by the icon displayed in Figure 1.4.

The Bloom's taxonomy cognitive domain (Bloom et al., 1956) points to analysis and evaluation, which collaborative partners need to discuss to carry them out together. They must be able to respectfully convey factual, conceptual, and procedural knowledge as well as perspectives and insights. Dialogue also entails the ability and personal characteristics associated with active listening. Being prepared, staying on topic, and responding thoughtfully are also important when the collaborative group depends on each member's contributions. Additional considerations are needed when some or all of the communication occurs online, including the timing for responses working asynchronously.

The third essential process for collaboration is *review*. This term is used to describe steps involved with providing critiques and feedback between participants who share and meld ideas, background research, or contributions to accomplish an assignment together. When review is structured with mutually acceptable boundaries and set criteria, participants provide objective perspectives on each other's work to exchange and transfer knowledge. In addition to the skills used in dialogue, review also allows participants to develop and use higher order thinking skills by analyzing, evaluating, and making judgments about the quality and relevance of their partners' contributions. They organize and integrate information into classification schemes.

The affective domain also comes into play during the review process because students learn respectful ways to respond to the phenomena that emerge when partners' work does not meet quality standards. Students can learn and develop values associated with ethical review practices. When the review process is carried out electronically, students can develop ICT competencies, such as the ability to work with attachments or use shared document tools to enter comments and track changes. Review is represented by the icon displayed in Figure 1.5.

Participants can organize a shared task in a variety of ways. A common way is described here as *parallel collaboration*. When a project is completed by a group using a parallel structure, tasks are allocated among participants. Parallel collaboration typically involves creating discrete individual pieces, and, through a process of dialogue and review, contributions are integrated into the final assignment deliverable. These learning experiences align with Bloom's cognitive processes for understanding and applying procedural knowledge as well as the factual and conceptual knowledge associated with the assignment itself. Parallel collaboration is represented by the icon displayed in Figure 1.6.

Figure 1.5. Review.

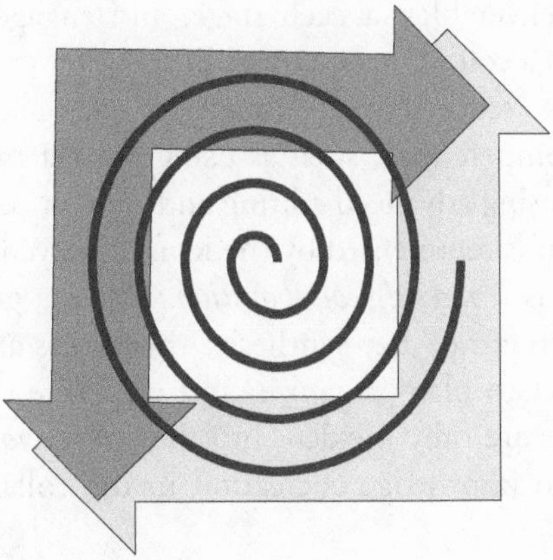

Figure 1.6. Parallel collaboration.

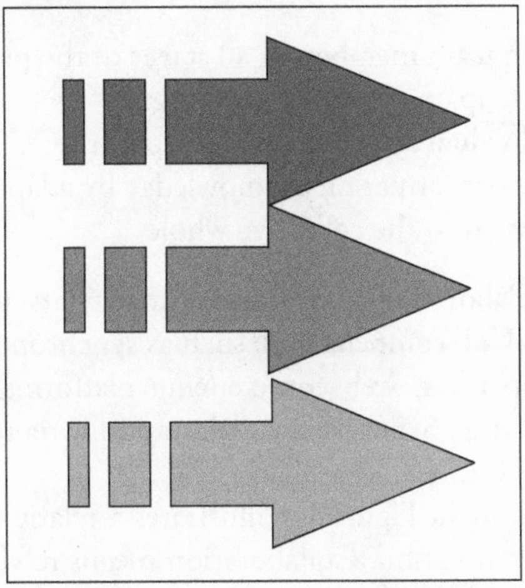

Sometimes a project has a temporal basis, which means it is completed in multiple steps over time. This way to organize a collaborative process is termed *sequential collaboration*. When a collaborative group uses a sequential structure to complete a project, components of the project are organized into a series of progressive steps, and results are combined into one collective product. Each step may involve individual work as well as collective work by a subgroup. Participants determine how each contribution is integrated into the final product through a process of dialogue and peer review. In addition to the competencies for coordination, quality control, and accountability utilized in parallel structures, through sequential collaboration, participants can learn to coordinate timing and multistep processes, use quality control criteria to assess deliverables at each stage, and engage members from all stages in creation of a collective outcome. In addition to ICT skills described for previous levels, sequential collaboration also allows participants to develop and use competencies, such as using project management tools to track progress and using advanced editing and version control software functions. Collaboration is represented by the icon displayed in Figure 1.7.

The final level is *synergistic collaboration*. When a group of participants uses a synergistic structure, they synthesize their ideas and work through all stages of the project to plan, organize, and complete the project together. Their contributions are fully melded into the collective final product. This level corresponds to knowledge cocreation in the collaborative knowledge learning model.

In addition to the group process and procedural competencies described previously, through synergistic collaboration participants can learn to do the following:

- Interact with team members at all stages of the project.
- Practice participatory decision-making.
- Balance individual interests with group purpose.
- Generate new information or knowledge by adapting and integrating multiple parts into the collective whole.

Synergistic collaboration also allows participants to develop and use digital literacy and ICT competencies, such as synchronous communication and shared desktop tools, web conferencing platforms for meetings, and live writing and editing. Synergistic collaboration is represented by the icon displayed in Figure 1.8.

The vertical arrow in Figure 1.1 illustrates a relationship between trust and the level of collaboration. Collaboration means relying on others' abilities and integrity and being confident that the other learner(s) can and will share your commitment toward meeting the learning goal of the assignment. As illustrated in the taxonomy (Figure 1.1.), as the processes of collaboration

Figure 1.7. Sequential collaboration.

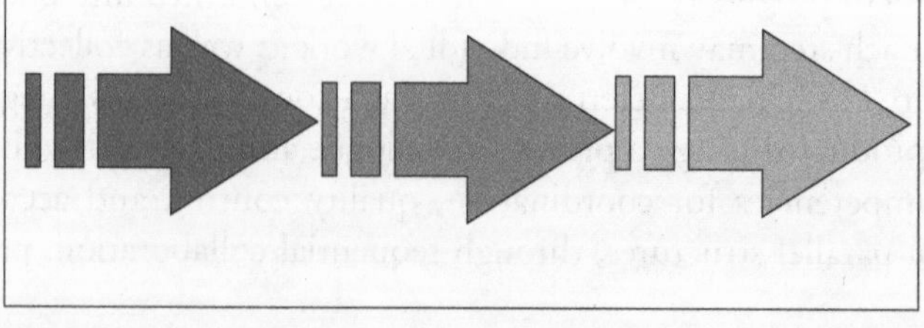

Figure 1.8. Synergistic collaboration.

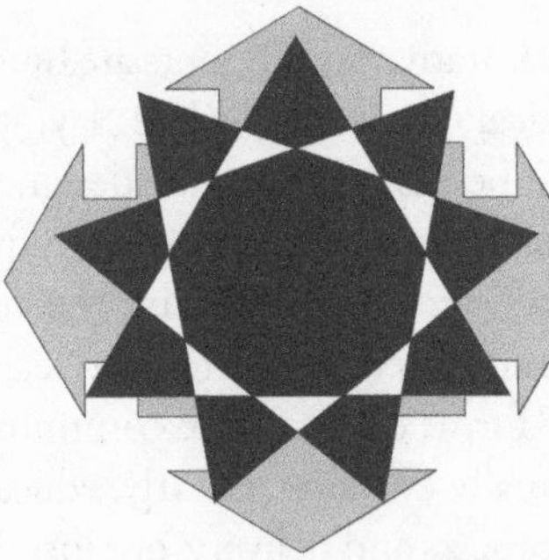

become more complex and the levels of collaboration increase, so does the need for increasingly deeper levels of trust. The reciprocal loyalties and common purpose needed for successful collaborative learning involve trust not only among the student partners but also between the instructor and the students and the learners and the institution. The taxonomy of collaboration encourages development of trust through purposeful assignments with clear expectations and fair assessments.

Using Taxonomies to Structure Assignments

When an educator creates a learning experience with guiding principles from Bloom's taxonomies, learners are encouraged to pursue multiple goals through that experience. They can develop competencies in the content area, while learning how to think critically and connect the work at hand with their own values and passions. When an educator creates collaborative learning activities with the knowledge learning model in mind, she thinks about the purpose of working together. When an educator creates a learning experience with guiding principles from the taxonomy of collaboration, learners are encouraged to pursue multiple goals through that experience such as acquiring competencies in the content area and skills in reflection and communication, while learning how to lead, manage, and make decisions with a group process. If the learning experience occurs electronically, learners can also develop proficiencies with practical use of ICT. Each element of the taxonomy of collaboration is explored in depth in coming chapters. Part Three of this book provides recommendations for how to use the taxonomy in the design of assignments and assessments. By integrating ideas from all of these frameworks, educators create opportunities for meaningful learning that aligns with curricular requirements and prepares students for success in academic and professional contexts.

New Skills in Collaboration . . . for Faculty, Too!

Educators who create collaborative assignments are building on well-established theoretical and pedagogical traditions while laying the groundwork for educational innovations. When assignments are designed for completion by collaborative partners, the objective is for peers to learn from and with each other within parameters and milieux determined by the instructor. Collaborative, cooperative, team, peer, and other styles of social learning are not new—but with the advent of diverse forms of electronic communications, the ways social learning occurs are continually evolving. Clearly, educators have new responsibilities to think about for process and delivery, not just the content of the course.

Not very long ago, the role of a faculty member in a university was a fairly independent one. Professors were entirely responsible for the development and delivery of their courses. At research institutions, credentials and merit for tenure and promotions were not derived from excellence in teaching. Faculty members were retained because they were leading subject matter experts in their respective fields, not for their ability to teach the subject.

Now even the most traditional institutions offer courses online or through blended approaches in which face-to-face classes are complemented with online materials and assignments. Not only are new styles of teaching and learning necessary but the whole process of curriculum and course development has changed. Increasingly, a wide range of people, including academic leaders, faculty, subject matter experts, editors and copyright coordinators, media developers, assessment specialists, instructional designers, and instructional technologists, work together to design curricula. In some cases, the curriculum or course may involve more than one disciplinary field, making the development team multidisciplinary as well as cross-functional. The previously independent faculty member and diverse professionals must learn to collaborate—and most likely at least some of the collaborative process will occur online. These shifts mean not only that today's faculty members create the environments where learners can collaborate but also that their roles *with* learners are also more collaborative. Today's faculty members benefit from sophisticated ICT literacy and online collaboration skills. Educators who see these trends develop an enlarged repertoire of approaches to teaching and learning.

With changing roles, it is useful to clarify the terms used in this book. Sometimes faculty members carry out all of these roles to design and teach their students with collaborative approaches. Other times professionals work together to create a course that is delivered by one or more instructors.

- The instructional designer recommends or chooses the platform and features used in the learning activity, project, and assignments. Individuals in these roles are referred to as the *designers*.

- The subject matter expert is responsible for providing content that corresponds with the goals and objectives of the curriculum as a whole or the specific course. Individuals in these roles are referred to as the *SMEs*.
- The instructor or facilitator teaches students and carries out the learning activity, project, or assignment. Individuals in these roles are referred to here as *instructors*.
- The term *educators* is used to encompass these roles more generally, including those who design, contribute subject matter expertise, teach, and assess student learning.

Additional terms used in this book are briefly defined here:

- The students or learners who work and learn together are described as *collaborative partners*.
- The umbrella term *assignments* encompasses any kind of student work. Stand-alone exercises, typically completed in one or two class sessions, are referred to as a single *learning activity*. Multistage assignments that include a series of learning activities, completed over a longer time frame, are referred to as *projects*. Projects can include both collaborative and solo assignments and can be evaluated on both individual and collective bases.
- Collaborative partners work as a part of a *group* on short-term assignments or single learning activities. Partners committed to longer-term projects can be considered members of a *team*. However, for the sake of clarity, the term *group* is used to describe two or more partners who are collaborating.

New Directions for Collaborating in Twenty-First-Century Milieux

The usefulness of collaborative competencies extends beyond the classroom. Work life is rarely a solo activity; we need to work together to get things done. Although many of us would like to think we act primarily as individuals in organizations, this is rarely the case. In many types of positions, we frequently work with groups, and in many cases, we are expected to build true teams in which individuals are expected to possess a strong commitment to shared goals and demonstrate a high degree of group cohesion and regard for one another. Even when group members know how to collaborate and are confident about working successfully in groups, the wider organization must additionally ensure that support systems (e.g., policies, practices, processes, and technologies) are aligned with their efforts. By learning about the factors that support collaborative practice, students will be able to look and act in ways that are productive for all involved.

To succeed in the workplace of tomorrow, today's students need opportunities to develop twenty-first-century skills that will allow them to work collaboratively across boundaries of geography, time, and culture. Professional life in the age of the Internet requires a different set of strategic, cross-cultural, team, and technical skills than did the face-to-face operations of the past. We need to communicate to work together, to know when to use which technology, and to realize when we need time together to build or rebuild trust. It takes knowledge, self-reflection, and practice to learn how to form and manage collaborative groups.

Assignments completed collaboratively allow students to learn these skills and develop a repertoire of approaches that align with an active role in a networked society and economy. Those who are preparing today's students for the future help them by incorporating a variety of collaborative approaches into both the content and process of educational activities. The knowledge learning model, Bloom's taxonomies, and the taxonomy of collaboration offer educators new and classic models that focus on collaboration and learning in today's connected milieu. These flexible models are designed to help educators match different types of collaboration to their own circumstances and assess successful participation. Circumstances that might affect choice of collaborative assignment include the task, curricular purpose, participant characteristics, existing relationships and trust among members, available time frame, and desired outcomes. Circumstances that might affect choice of online collaborative style include participants' experience with using electronic technologies for communicating with diverse collaborative partners to make agreements, plans, and decisions and to coordinate their efforts.

Key Questions: Prompts for Discussion or Reflection

- Reflect on the premises of this book. Do you think it is important for students to learn how to collaborate? Why or why not?
- How would you compare and contrast the knowledge learning model, Bloom's taxonomy, and the taxonomy of collaboration? How could principles and constructs of the three models be used together?
- What part(s) of the collaborative process have you experienced in academic or professional life? What are your observations about what worked or didn't work? How could you organize the process differently?

- How would you decide when working collaboratively is appropriate versus when working individually is appropriate?
- Based on your experiences, what are the most challenging aspects of working collaboratively? What would you recommend to improve the collaborative process and the quality of the outcomes?

2

THEORETICAL FOUNDATIONS FOR COLLABORATIVE LEARNING

True teachers are those who use themselves as bridges over which they invite their students to cross; then, having facilitated their crossing, joyfully collapse, encouraging them to create their own.

—Nikos Kazantzakis, 2005

Objectives

Chapter 2 will prepare you to:

- Identify positions related to social models of instruction and learning offered by educational theories, frameworks, and models.
- Summarize key theoretical constructs that explain principles essential to collaborative learning.
- Understand and apply principles of e-social constructivism in the context of your own work as an educator.

Introduction

Theories, frameworks, and models show us the ways scholars have thought about and analyzed the processes of teaching and learning. They are the basis of scholarly research design and writing. They can also serve practical purposes for educators who want to utilize new instructional approaches, because we can reference respected theoretical and conceptual writings to add credibility to our own proposals. In chapter 1, four different taxonomies or models were introduced: the collaborative knowledge learning model, Bloom's taxonomies for the cognitive and affective domains, and the taxonomy of collaboration. They draw or build on constructivist and social constructivist theories, theories of collaboration, and emerging models and frameworks describing learning networks and communities. While a full review of these theories is beyond the scope of this book, a survey of major constructs raises key questions we need to consider as we design and teach with collaborative methods. Finally, a synthesis of theoretical constructs with recommendations drawn from interviews with instructors and my own teaching experience is used to generate a proposed theory of e-social constructivism. This proposed theory takes into consideration the potential for using technology in the instructional setting itself and the ways educators and students communicate when they collaborate.

Constructivism

Contemporary literature and practice in education and instructional design have long drawn on constructivist theories to describe the importance of active, rather than receptive, models of teaching and learning. A core notion of constructivism is that knowledge has a subjective dimension because people construct meaning based on their own interpretations. Each individual student discovers meanings based on his or her perceptions, experiences, and prior knowledge. From a constructivist educator's perspective, it is not possible to impose meaning; instead, our roles involve creating and facilitating learning activities and assignments that allow students to make their own discoveries.

Constructivist learning environments require student work that is intrinsically motivating to them; learners reaching a certain level of self-directedness; and teachers who provide support (scaffolding), context, relevance, and constant feedback. In these environments learners are encouraged to build on prior knowledge, think critically, reflect, and present their information independently and in small groups. As students' capacity increases, they become responsible for both the content and process of learning, which frees up the teacher to play a nonexpert, facilitator, or guiding role (Cattaneo, 2017).

Some theorists were not satisfied with this focus on individuals and suggested that learners do not make sense of content on their own. Social constructivism focuses on the potential for learning that occurs when meanings are constructed through experiences that involve two or more students. From a social constructivist educator's perspective, knowledge is not simply constructed, it is coconstructed. Constructivist and social constructivist theories have their roots in the thinking of Dewey, Piaget, Vygotsky, and Bruner.

Foundational research on social or peer learning was conducted before the advent of the Internet, or with subjects who collaborated in face-to-face classrooms (Oakley, Felder, Brent, & Elhajj, 2004; Yazici, 2004). The often cited research by Vygotsky was conducted with K–12 schoolchildren (Vygotsky, 1978, 1987). Contemporary interpretations aim to bring these ideas into the digital age when students use ICTs to connect, whether they are studying in the same physical classroom or in online learning management systems with students from across the globe. The community of inquiry framework developed by Anderson and Garrison explains the importance of presence in e-learning (Garrison, 2017; Rourke, Garrison, Anderson, & Archer, 2000)

Three additional models offer lenses through which we will critique these theories: Joseph Schwab's (1983) learning commonplaces and Salmons's instructor roles continuum and knowledge learning model, as described in this book. Taken together, these models provide terms we can use to explain the practical implications of theoretical constructs about roles and expectations for educators and students within a particular curriculum and learning environment, so we can decide which ones fit our particular circumstances for designing, teaching, and assessing collaborative learning.

Finally, three schools of thought drawn from disciplines outside the field of education provide lenses through which to view collaboration in the context of teaching and learning. Theories of collaboration can help us to better understand the ways that social learning might be organized and carried out. The first theory is the theory of collaborative advantage, which suggests that there are outcomes that can be attained through collaborative effort that could not be attained by any of the players acting alone (Hibbert & Huxham, 2010; Huxham, 2003; Huxham & Vangen, 2004, 2005). The second theory is the theory of discursive collaboration, which asserts that conversation and collective identity are essential to achievement of such outcomes (Lotia & Hardy, 2008; Phillips & Hardy, 2002). The third theory encompasses social learning theory and social network theory, which provide us with a language to describe various ways people or "actors" in a collaborative "system" develop self-efficacy and relate to one another to learn (Bandura, 1977, 1986, 1997).

How can the premises and definitions articulated in these theories inform our efforts as educators to design, teach, and assess learning activities that are appropriate for the content and student characteristics? A brief overview provides a foundation for a set of principles that help us decide which options best fit the needs of our students.

Constructivism and Social Constructivism

When learning activities expect individuals to investigate, discover, and construct new meanings, they actualize *cognitive constructivist principles*. When learning activities expect groups of students to exchange and explore ideas together, they embody *social constructivist principles*.

John Dewey: Progressive Education

John Dewey's work set the stage for social constructivism. Dewey (1916) wrote at the advent of the Industrial Age and observed the potential of the railroad and telegraph to "eliminate distance between peoples and classes previously hemmed off from one another" (p. 85). He predicted that new forms of educative community would emerge because new connections would be made between people who previously had limited access to one another. "Persons do not become a society by living in physical proximity . . . . A book or a letter may institute a more intimate association between human beings separated thousands of miles from each other than exists between dwellers under the same roof" (Dewey, 1916, p. 4). Dewey foresaw the potential, as well as the challenges, new communications would bring to established ways of thinking and learning.

Dewey believed that learning occurs by "constant reorganizing or reconstructing of experience which adds to the meaning of experience, and which increases ability to direct the course of subsequent experience" (Dewey, 1916, p. 76). Dewey's writings about education were based on the premise that learning is a social function, with a central principle of *interaction.* He described interaction between the student and teacher, between the student and the situation, and among students (Dewey, 1916, 1938). Dewey recommended that learners actively participate in learning situations outside the classroom, equating the community to the laboratory—a place to experiment (Dewey, 1938).

Jean Piaget: Sociocognitive Constructivism

Jean Piaget was a pioneer in child development and child psychology. He was especially concerned with the development of children's logical thinking capabilities (Piaget, 1952). Piaget's sociocognitive constructivism theory hypothesized that students learn when they create, adapt, and refine knowledge (Piaget, 1971). Students create knowledge structures and mental models through experience and observation (Talja, Tuominen, & Savolainen, 2004). Like Dewey, Piaget believed that individuals must construct their meaning through experiences that they can abstract into conceptual frameworks or schema of the world (Maraon, Benarroch, & Gaomez, 2000). The educator's task is to help students move from their inaccurate ideas and schemas toward conceptions more in consonance with what has been validated by disciplinary communities (Windschitl, 2002). While sociocognitive constructivism is primarily concerned with the individual's learning, Piaget saw peer interactions as crucial to a child's affective development and construction of social and moral feelings, values, and social and intellectual competence (DeVries, 1997).

Lev Vygotsky: Sociocultural Constructivism

Lev Vygotsky is credited with being the foundational thinker for sociocultural constructivism. From the perspective of this school of thought, knowledge is a cultural product. Vygotsky saw a causal relationship between social interaction and individual cognitive change (Dillenbourg, Baker, Blaye, & O'Malley, 1996, 1999; Vygotsky, 1978). He argued that learning involves both interpsychological and intrapsychological language functions. Learning requires communication and social exchange with others as well as inner speech used to reflect and think.

Vygotsky is best known for his conception of a zone of proximal development (ZPD), describing the distance between what one can do alone and what can be accomplished in collaboration with others who are more capable (Vygotsky, 1978). This is also called *appropriation* because a learner appropriates strategies used by a teacher, parent, or more experienced learner. When one learner is more knowledgeable than the other, it is expected that the latter learns from the former. However, researchers have discovered that when students work together, learning extends to the more able peer, the knowledgeable other, and he or she also benefits from the interaction.

Vygotsky viewed the teacher as the one to orchestrate meaningful, "whole" activities, constructive tasks, or problem-solving situations, through which more knowledgeable learners can assist others. Constructive tasks, such as conducting scientific inquiries, solving mathematical problems, and creating and interpreting literary texts, are contrasted with decontextualized skill-building (Windschitl, 2002).

Jerome Bruner: Discovery and Spiral Learning

By the time Jerome Bruner started to write about education in the 1960s, the theories developed by Dewey, Piaget, and Vygotsky were well known. Bruner built on their work and looked at ways constructivism could inform curriculum design as well as the organization of class activities. He outlined three steps of the learning process: acquisition of new information; transformation of the new information to fit new tasks; and evaluation, which takes place when learners check whether the new information is adequate to the task. He did not see these as discrete steps, but as part of a spiral, in which learning continues to build and evolve through interactions with new ideas and people (Bruner, 1966, 1971, 1977, 1986, 1990; Bruner & Kearsley, 2004). The concept of spiral curriculum inspired the practice called *scaffolding*. Scaffolding is described by Wood, Bruner, and Ross (1976) as "controlling those elements of the task that are initially beyond the learner's capability thus permitting him to concentrate upon and complete only those elements that are within his range of competence" (p. 90).

According to Bruner, scaffolding is most effective when learners and educators iteratively communicate their growing understandings. With respect to collaborative learning, at least two classes of scaffolds can be distinguished: scaffolds that provide support on a content-related or conceptual level and scaffolds that provide support related to the interactive processes between the collaborators.

Contemporary Interpretations of Social Constructivism

Albert Bandura: Social Learning Theory

Social learning theory explains human behavior in terms of continuous reciprocal interaction among cognitive, behavioral, and environmental influences. Albert Bandura (1977, 1986) termed this interaction *reciprocal determinism.* He formulated the following four-stage process:

1. Attention: The individual notices something in the environment.
2. Retention: The individual remembers what was noticed.
3. Reproduction: The individual produces an action that is a copy of what was noticed.
4. Motivation: The environment delivers a consequence that changes the probability the behavior will be repeated through reinforcement or punishment.

The basic principles proposed by Bandura are that people learn by observing others and that learning can occur without an observable change in behavior. Cognition plays a role in learning, with attention as the critical factor. Modeling teaches new behaviors, may influence the frequency of previously learned behaviors, and may also encourage previously forbidden behaviors. The model may be a *live model,* the actual person, or a *symbolic model* portrayed in print or media.

Moshman and Geil: Exogenous, Dialectical, and Endogenous Constructivism

Types of social constructivism exist on a continuum, according to a model offered by David Moshman and Molly Geil (Moshman, 1997; Moshman & Geil, 1998). Exogenous constructivism emphasizes that "external" knowledge is best taught through direct instruction, in conjunction with exercises requiring learners to be cognitively active. Dialectical constructivism proposes that learning occurs through realistic experience, but that learners require *scaffolding* provided by teachers or experts as well as collaboration with peers. Endogenous constructivism emphasizes the individual nature of each learner's knowledge construction process and suggests that the role of the teacher should be to act as a facilitator in providing experiences that are likely to result in challenges to learners' existing models.

Prawat: Ideas-Based Social Constructivism

This version changes the focus from learning through practical problem-solving to direct encounters with ideas. Richard Prawat (1993) suggests that curriculum be thought of as a matrix of "big ideas" (p. 13). Teachers serve as "managers or orchestrators" (p. 13) who work alongside students as they explore ideas together (Prawat, 1993).

Rodriguez and Berryman: Sociotransformative Constructivism

Multicultural education is merged with social constructivism, providing an "orientation to teaching and learning that pays close attention to how issues of power, gender, and equity influence not only what subject matter (curriculum) is covered but also how it is taught and to whom" (Rodriguez & Berryman, 2002, p. 1019). Alberto J. Rodriguez and Chad Berryman point to the concept of *agency*, which bridges knowledge and transformative action. They believe that agency can lead to a deeper understanding of the subject matter and to the application of newly gained knowledge in socially relevant ways (Rodriguez & Berryman, 2002; Zozakiewicz & Rodriguez, 2007).

Von Glasersfeld: Radical Constructivism

Radical constructivism and the theory of rational knowing was championed by Ernst Von Glasersfeld, who observed that the world beyond our experiential interface may show us what concepts, theories, and actions are not viable, but it cannot instruct us what to think (Glasersfeld, 1996). Radical constructivists believe teachers or facilitators should provide limited support, and learners should construct their own mental models within the environment that exemplifies the topics being studied (Dalgarno, 2001).

Theories of Collaboration

Theories from fields and disciplines beyond education offer insights that help us to better understand the collaborative process.

Theory of Collaborative Advantage

According to this theory, collaboration involves a tension between two forces, collaborative advantage and collaborative inertia (Hibbert & Huxham, 2005; Huxham, 2003; Huxham & Vangen, 2001; Vangen & Huxham, 2003). Collaborative advantage refers to the synergistic outcomes that could not have been achieved by any player acting alone. Huxham discusses the need for collaborative partners to negotiate how they will define shared objectives, navigate power differentials, build trust, and define leadership in order to achieve unique and valuable outcomes. *Collaborative inertia* refers to factors that impede progress or obstruct collaborations from achieving desired outcomes (Hibbert & Huxham, 2005; Huxham, 2003; Huxham & Vangen, 2001; Vangen & Huxham, 2003). Hansen and Nohria discovered that what Huxham calls *inertia* involves four specific barriers: unwillingness to seek input and learn from others; inability to seek and find expertise; unwillingness to help, also called hoarding expertise; and inability to work together and transfer knowledge (Hansen, 2009; Hansen & Nohria, 2004). Kouzes and Posner (2017) describe the impulse to compete as the chief barrier to collaboration. The theory of collaborative advantage seeks to explain ways the benefits of collaboration can be achieved and ways inertia and other barriers can be overcome.

Social Network Theory

Social network theory "focuses on the joint activities of, and continual exchanges between, participants in a social system" (Kenis & Oerlemans, 2008, p. 289). In particular, social network theory explores the "relationship patterns that connect the actors that make up a system's social structure" (p. 289). Wasserman and Faust (1994) identified key assumptions in social network theory including the following:

- Actors and their actions are viewed as interdependent rather than independent, autonomous units.
- Relational ties or linkages between actors are channels for transfer or flow of resources.
- *Structure* of the network refers to lasting patterns of relations among actors. The network structure may provide opportunities or constraints on individual actions.
- Social networks consist of a finite set or sets of actors and their relations.

Relational ties can include evaluation of other actors, transactions, transfers of resources, or behavioral interactions (e.g., talking). Social network theorists study relational ties among members of dyads, triads, subgroups (subsets of groups), or groups (Wasserman & Faust, 1994, p. 19). Network analysis allows researchers to study the structure of relations among actors in the network and the consequences for individuals in the network and the system as a whole (Kenis & Oerlemans, 2008).

While some researchers use social network theories to create algebraic or statistical models, the principles may also apply to qualitative studies of collaborative actors, systems, and relational ties. Network analysis looks at social units and provides a flexible set of concepts and models that can be used for interdisciplinary research. The related idea of *social capital* (Alfred, 2009; Hahapiet, 2008)—a measure of the value and benefit to an actor of the network connections—is also of use to researchers who want to understand characteristics of collaborative relationships.

Theory of Discourse and Collaboration

Another theory to consider draws our attention to the communication processes that collaborative partners use. According to this theory, collaboration depends on conversations among collaborators and on wider discourse with other stakeholders (Hardy, Lawrence, & Grant, 2005; Lotia & Hardy, 2008; Simonin, 2003). Collaboration from this view is a "social accomplishment that occurs in an iterative fashion over time" (Hardy et al., 2005, p. 59). Participants engage in *deliberative dialogue*, which is distinct from other kinds of discourse. Collaboration builds on specific communication patterns, described as a two-stage model. The first stage highlights the importance of a discursively constructed collective identity (Hardy et al., 2005). A collective identity "names" the group and allows participants to "construct themselves, the problem and the solution as part of the collaborative framework in which the potential for joint action is both significant and beneficial" (p. 63). The process of naming is critical as a step from individual to collective thinking. Common constructions facilitate communication and allow participants to create an atmosphere of mutual understanding (Hardy et al., 2005). Hardy and colleagues (2005) describe this process in terms of negotiating multiple stakes in the outcomes of the collaboration among individual stakeholders. Huxham similarly discusses learning about partners and their interest in the outcomes of the collaboration as critical to engagement in the collaborative process (Hibbert & Huxham, 2005).

Hardy and colleagues (2005) theorize that the second stage is where collective identity is translated into "synergistic and innovative action" (p. 59). This stage entails "constructions of key issues . . . in which central issues are defined in conversation" (p. 65). Two kinds of constructions define issues: common constructions negotiated and agreed upon with participants and private constructions that allow individuals to make sense of and express issues in their own terms. The "social accomplishment" of collaboration can generate strategic, political, and knowledge creation effects. Strategic effects are the potential to build organizational capacity. Political effects refer to changes in networks, relationships, and patterns of resource and information flows. Knowledge effects are the transfer of knowledge from one collaborative partner to another, as well as the potential to create new knowledge not previously understood by partners (Simonin, 2003).

A Comparative Analysis of Social Constructivist and Collaboration Theories

These theorists explored a wide range of pedagogic and philosophical questions. Positions represented in this set of theories are mapped using situational analysis tools. Positional maps provide a framework to visualize major positions taken in the data (Clarke, Fries, & Washburn, 2018). One focus is on the ways each theory describes or recommends roles and expectations for educators and students within the learning milieu. Since this analysis is not discipline specific, content issues are not addressed. The second focus is on the ways each theory describes the potential for learning by transferring, exchanging, acquiring, or cocreating knowledge.

Relationships among theories reviewed in this chapter, with respect to the two dimensions of learning style and instructional style, are mapped in Figure 2.1. This map provides a reference for understanding e-social learning theory in relation to earlier theories.

The vertical axis represents a continuum from the individual to the group as the focus of learning.

- In the bottommost position, the focus is on the individual's learning experience.
- In the middle position, the individual's learning is catalyzed by the social process with the group.
- In the topmost position, the group is the focus with learning through interactions with peers and instructors.

The horizontal axis shows a continuum of instructional styles from instructor to learner driven.

- In the leftmost position, an instructor organizes and sequences content to convey information through direct instruction.
- In the middle position, an instructor facilitates learning by organizing and scaffolding assignments. The instructor shares knowledge, clarifies expectations and parameters, and keeps learners on topic and on task. The instructor is flexible and provides guidance as needed.
- In the rightmost position, an instructor provides minimal guidance. Learners discover, contribute, or generate knowledge independently.

Figure 2.1. Situational map of constructivist positions.

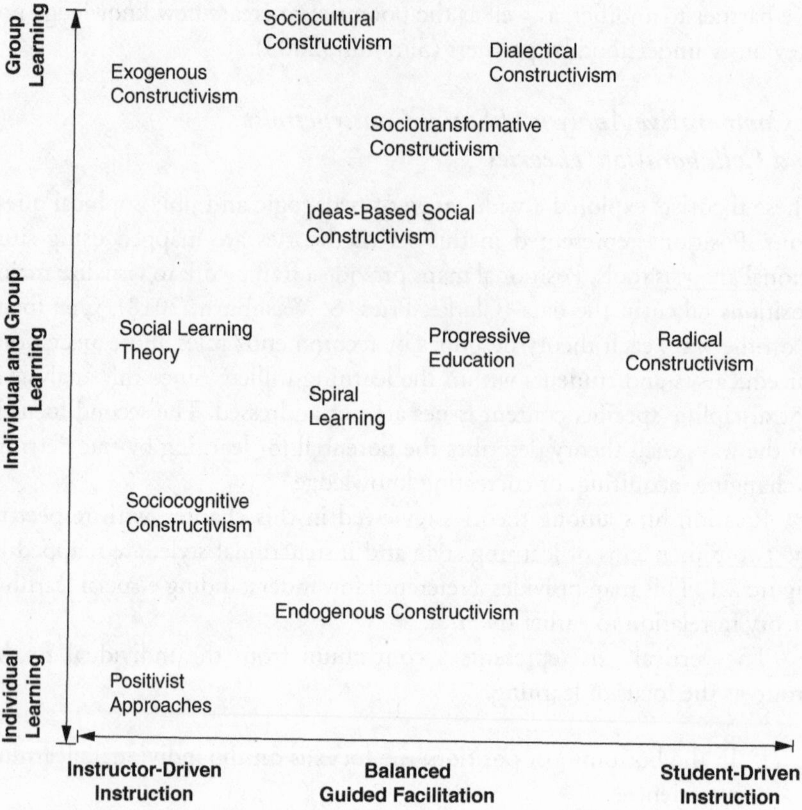

As illustrated, constructivist positions are quite literally all over the map. While many of the theories encompass group learning in some way, surprisingly, many of them support an instructor-driven, direct-instruction mode.

The Taxonomy of Collaboration and a Theory of e-Social Constructivism

Given the comparison of categories in the theoretical literature and the practical experiences described in the interview data, I propose *e-social constructivism* as an updated educational theory. Since this theory aims to contribute to the improvement of teaching and learning, it can be described as an instructional theory. Educational theories can be classified as either learning theories or instructional theories. According to Jerome Bruner (1996) theories of learning are descriptive, while theories of instruction are prescriptive. Learning theories describe, after the fact, how people learn. Theories of instruction recommend the most effective way of designing and conducting instructional activities so learners acquire the knowledge or skill (Morrison, Ross, & Kemp, 2004). A theory of instruction is concerned with improving rather than describing learning.

Views From the Field

Most theorists are not confronted with the messy realities of the classroom, but these realities need to be considered when we try to articulate some guiding principles that will be helpful to educators who design, plan, and teach. Interview questions were posed to elicit perspectives about what instructional strategies the instructors used and what they considered *success* in terms of sustained student engagement throughout all stages of the collaborative assignment and student ability to participate and contribute to the activity, as well as achievement of curricular objectives. I also draw on my own teaching experience and observations. Three broad categories that represent this mix of experiences are (a) knowledge and skills needed to teach with collaborative methods, (b) instructor commitment to collaboration, and (c) instructional situation.

Knowledge and Skills Needed to Teach With Collaborative Methods

Instructors who participated in my research identified kinds of knowledge and skills they felt were essential for educators who teach using collaborative methods in online or hybrid settings. Throughout this section, quoted material is from research participants' responses unless otherwise noted. Responses were categorized into the following areas:

- Understand the new paradigm: To be effective in designing and guiding collaborative learning, instructors need updated practical and theoretical understandings about teaching and learning in ways that are active, student driven, and collaborative. A research participant observed, "In order for faculty and students to succeed, [they] need to get the sense of working in [a] different paradigm. [There is a] need for bridging theory and application."
- Be an advocate: Instructors need to be able to advocate the benefits of collaborative learning and overcome resistance and other barriers. A research participant asserted, "[The instructor] must be the enabler to get the collaboration done, the 'driver' to push the things."
- Model collaborative behaviors: The best way that instructors drive productive collaborative behaviors is by modeling them. One instructor said, "I make sure I am modeling openness and experimentation, being an equal learner with others in the class."

- Have skills in online communication and facilitation: Research participants spoke at length about what they considered the most essential skills: online communication and facilitation. Given the potential for dispersed class members to feel isolated, a research participant observed that, while in a face-to-face lecture it is not necessary for instructors to know learners, in an online class they interact one-on-one. Another research participant described the importance of using people skills online: being sensitive, patient, and able to "show concern and guidance as needed, with a nurturing style."

Instructor Commitment to Collaboration

Research participants believed it is critically important for instructors to be committed to collaborative methods and prepared to take varied individual and group actions to facilitate collaborative activities. All respondents made the point that, for online collaboration to successfully occur, the instructor must be prepared to take an active role. Laying the groundwork for interaction between instructor and learners as well as among learners requires careful attention. They described three key responsibilities for instructors.

The first responsibility is designing, planning, and structuring learning activities. Study participants emphasized the value of well-planned learning activities. While in some cases the assignments are already in place as part of an online class design, instructional choices remain. Research participants emphasized that successful collaboration happens when online learners trust each other and trust the process. Several research participants pointed out that when the work is structured into stages, students can focus on the task and course content without being overwhelmed by the process. Participants recommended that the instructor direct the approach in the early stages of collaboration and increasingly put responsibility into students' hands. The instructor begins by assessing learners' readiness for collaboration and makes choices about how, when, and to what extent responsibility can shift to the learners. According to learners who participated in this study, the instructor can gradually "allow learners to build on or suggest options so learners cocreate the next steps." Instructors "provide a framework so students can focus on the task. Define clearly the time limits, geographic or conceptual limits of the task." The instructor should work to "move students toward being autonomous and self-organized but, initially, show them how to participate." Research participants were in consensus that expectations and specific instructional guidelines help learners understand how to move from one stage of the collaborative process to another.

The second responsibility is being a learning coach. As instructors, research participants encourage critical thinking about learning, meta-thinking or meta-learning, and reflection. A research participant pointed out that instructors need to "be present but not present," to allow groups to solve their own problems and intervene only when the group cannot resolve a difficulty. Another participant made a similar suggestion, saying, "When there is discomfort, be silent, be there and listen. Listen before intervening."

In addition to group coaching, several research participants suggested that private coaching or one-to-one communication with a student is appropriate when the collaborative process is stuck. A student may benefit from the instructor's individual attention if that student falls behind or surges ahead. In either case, such learners can jeopardize the success of the group. A participant described a circumstance in which a highly motivated, capable learner works independently to complete an entire task, thereby disempowering the collaborative group and undercutting shared agreements and time lines. On the other end of the spectrum is the passive lurker, someone who is not pulling his or her weight. Instructors should intervene to explain relevant points about the collaborative process and motivate the learner to fulfill his or her responsibility to the team or encourage the team to review work agreements for completing the project. In such situations timely involvement of the instructor can help the group avoid getting sidetracked by group process.

The third responsibility is developing students' collaboration skills. A participant made the collaborative process part of the lesson: "It is extremely important to discuss the nature and value of collaboration before embarking." Several participants assigned regular and frequent partner work, then built up to the small group assignment. They provided suggestions for different roles people can take in collaborative groups and let students choose. They subsequently allowed learners to build on or suggest options so they gradually grew into cocreating activities.

In summary, at each stage these instructors took active, responsive roles to help learners structure, organize, and complete the collaborative activity. In the process, they sought to build learners' skills in collaboration as well as achievement of curricular goals.

Educational Milieu as "Situation"

John Dewey (1938) talked about learning as interaction involving students, teachers, content, and situation. Later Joseph Schwab (1983) used the term *commonplaces* to describe these four interrelated factors. The fourth commonplace, *situation*, differentiates the literature written about instruction in traditional face-to-face classrooms from the perceptions of those who teach in online or blended milieux. Online or hybrid instructors need to support development of trusting relationships, demonstrate presence to prevent isolation that would keep learners from engaging in social learning exchanges, help learners either develop skills or find technical support services necessary for participation when technologies are being used, and guide learners toward intellectual exchange and growth. An important conclusion based on this analysis of the theories in the context of instructional experience is that a radical hands-off interpretation of constructivism does not offer optimal presence necessary to support collaborative learning activities. At the same time, an instructor-driven approach, in which the roles and plans for the collaborative activity are provided to the students, would not invite students to learn how to collaborate. The students could acquire subject matter knowledge and benefit from social learning with peers, but they would not be prepared to plan and manage future collaborative projects.

Theory of E-Social Constructivism

The proposed theory of e-social constructivism recognizes the unique set of opportunities and limitations of the online or hybrid social and learning milieux. While student-centered, this theory recommends important roles for educators who endeavor to teach with collaborative methods. Leadership writers Kouzes and Posner (2017) point out that, "As paradoxical as it might seem, leadership is more essential—not less—when collaboration is required" (p. 79). The same might be said in the educational context, in which more instructional presence is needed for collaborative, in contrast to individual, online assignments. Thoughtful attention to structure, purpose, and guidance can result in collaborative e-learning that truly engages learners in construction of new meanings. Balance and flexibility are key: Sometimes direct instruction is needed on content or on how to use a web meeting platform. Other times the instructor needs to step back and let students act autonomously to make their own decisions.

Principles of E-Social Constructivism

Learning occurs through meaningful interaction with content, content experts (who may include instructors, authorities, or skilled practitioners), and peers. Learning is supported in electronic and face-to-face milieux that are conducive to social exchange and to exploration by both individuals and groups. The collaborative process and the subject matter that is the focus of collaborative activity both provide important context as learners construct meaning from their activities. Through collaborative learning activities, students can acquire new knowledge together with partners; exchange and appropriate knowledge through peer exchange; and create new, innovative knowledge, skills, and solutions. Instructors should understand and acknowledge that learners' prior experiences and cultural, institutional, and historical contexts influence individual and group accomplishment.

When courses are designed with social, collaborative activities, instructors must help learners avoid isolation and separation from the interactive process. Using the principles of scaffolding, instructors provide support and information that learners need to interact successfully in online milieux. Instructors' social and cognitive presence is essential to the success of learners and learning teams. Instructors should encourage learners to develop and use ICT beyond the social uses they are familiar with in order to develop higher levels of digital competencies, by integrating opportunities to develop progressively more complex online research, collaboration, and communication skills.

In Figure 2.2, the theory of e-social constructivism is placed in a central position in relation to other theories reviewed in this chapter. This position

Figure 2.2. E-social constructivism in a theoretical context.

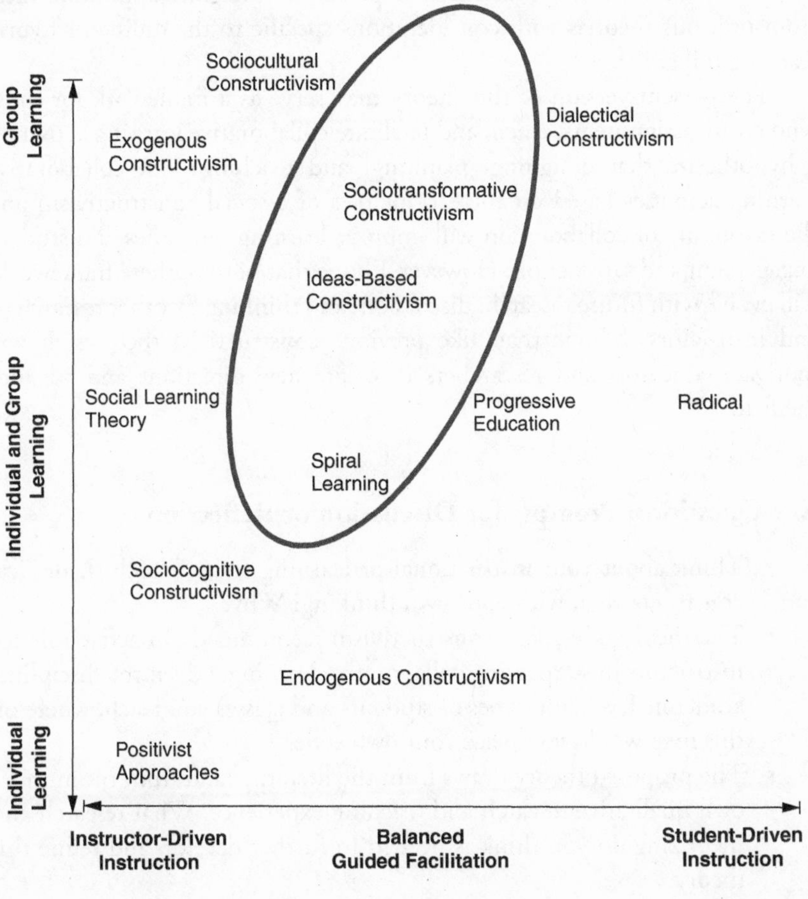

represents a balanced, guided facilitation role for instructors and a balance of individual and social learning. The theory acknowledges the interplay of individual and social constructions of knowledge, the need for internalized speech and reflection, and individual and collective contributions in the collaborative process.

Summary

This chapter presented a grounded theory and situational analysis of two sources: theoretical concepts from the literature and perceptions of educators who participated in a phenomenological study of collaborative e-learning. After comparing positions of various theorists with tested, practical ideas reported by constructivist online instructors, those ideas and positions most applicable to collaborative e-learning were integrated into a theory of e-social constructivism. E-social constructivist principles integrate applicable ideas from previous theories with considerations specific to the online or hybrid learning milieux.

The present version of this theory may serve as a framework for those who create assignments, teach, and facilitate collaborative learning activities. I hypothesize that designing, planning, and teaching with collaborative learning activities based on these principles of e-social constructivism and the taxonomy of collaboration will improve learning outcomes and student engagement and satisfaction. However, I hope that both of these frameworks will evolve with future research, discussion, and thinking by other researchers and instructors. I hope that, like previous constructivist theories, it will motivate educators and researchers to create new directions and advance the field.

Key Questions: Prompts for Discussion or Reflection

- Think about your instructional or learning style: Which theoretical constructs align with your own thinking? Why?
- The theory of e-social constructivism recommends an active role for instructors in supporting collaborative learning. Given the discipline, academic level, and types of students and classes you teach, where on this map would you place your own style?
- The proposed theory draws from the literature and from the author's own qualitative research and teaching experience. What research and theorizing do you think is needed to further develop and refine this theory?

PART TWO

UNDERSTANDING THE TAXONOMY OF COLLABORATION

3

TRUST AND COMMUNICATION IN THE COLLABORATIVE PROCESS

At the instructional level, promoting quality hinges on providing a design that stimulates and supports an engaging collaborative dialogue.

—Sorensen, Takle, & Moser, 2006

Objectives

Chapter 3 will prepare you to:

- Analyze types of trust.
- Understand types of communication.
- Create ways to build trust and foster productive communication with students who are engaged in collaborative assignments.
- Reflect on how you can model best communication and review practices in your role as an instructor.

Introduction

Part Three of this book offers guidance on ways to apply these ideas by designing assignments and assessing students. This chapter introduces three processes that are essential throughout a collaborative experience: building trust, communicating, and reviewing each other's work. Chapter 4 explores the ways to organize collaborative work.

Trust: The Glue That Keeps a Collaborative Group Together

Trust is not one element of the collaborative process; it is the most important element. Collaboration means reliance on others' abilities and integrity and confidence that the other student partners can and will share your commitment to meeting the learning goal of the assignment. Reciprocal loyalties and common purpose central to collaborative learning involve trust not only among the students but also between the instructor and the students.

When collaborative partners trust each other, they are willing to forgive small mistakes or missed deadlines. They are willing to put in extra effort for a partner who is having a bad week. These kinds of allowances for failures and tolerance for collaborative partners' minor shortcomings are described as "generous trust" by Obayashi, Inagaki, and Takikawa (2016). Generous partners are willing to take the time needed to guide someone who does not understand the task or needs to develop some additional skills to complete it. Trust, then, enables students to exchange, transfer, acquire, and cocreate knowledge together, as described in the collaborative knowledge learning model.

When collaborative partners do not trust each other, minor issues can be magnified and become fissures that tear the group apart. Partners might suspect that others are trying to get away with inadequate contribution, that they are not doing their fair share. Instead of feeling generous toward the other, they hold back and are reluctant to share what they know. Without trust, students are unable to engage in even the most basic level of learning exchange. These issues can be more difficult to resolve when the expectations or assignments are unclear or when the instructor is unavailable for consultation about interpersonal dynamics so essential to success. Bichard (2005) noted that "people will not take risks or use their initiative when they are not confident that support will be available when they need it. Nor will they share new, maybe surprising ideas with colleagues they do not trust" (p. 504).

While some people are predisposed to trust because of their open personalities or positive experiences, others use stereotypes as the basis of initial judgments of trustworthiness, and still others closely watch how collaborative partners behave before deciding on their trustworthiness (Ford, Piccolo, & Ford, 2017). Online, these prejudgments can be less damaging, when people have the chance to show responsiveness, or more damaging, when replies to e-mails or posts are delayed or are perceived as inadequate. By understanding the kinds of perspectives students might bring to the collaborative learning activity, we can better design and plan our instructional approach. (More on student characteristics and assignment design is discussed in chapter 5.)

Scholars offer multiple interpretations of what it means to trust the people and process when they are engaged in a collaboration. Charles Handy (1995), an early writer about the dynamics of technology-mediated communication, observed the need for more attention to trust in the virtual world in his predictive article "Trust and the Virtual Organization." He defined *trust* as "the confidence that a person is competent to reach a goal and is committed to reaching it" and observed that the practice of trust "implies reciprocal loyalty" (Handy, 1995, pp. 7–8). Others point to the willingness to be vulnerable as a defining characteristic of trust (Brown, Scott Poole, & Rodgers, 2004). Some point to a distinction between affective and cognitive trust. Affective trust is based on emotional ties formed between two parties in a relationship that results from the mutual exhibition of care and concern, while cognitive trust is based on an evaluation of salient characteristics such as integrity, competence, reliability, and dependability (Zhu, Newman, Miao, & Hooke, 2013). To simplify the types described in the literature and focus on those most applicable to teaching and learning, we will categorize them as personal, strategic, and organizational trust.

Personal Trust

Personal trust refers to individuals' willingness to open themselves to one another and to rely on collaborative partners' abilities and integrity. In the collaborative learning context, personal trust can be explored in the relationships and interactions of all involved: instructor–student and student–student. In service-learning, practica, or field-based studies, trust is a part of the student–community representative relationship. Trusting partners are confident that together they can and will commit to meeting the learning goal(s) of the assignment. Personal trust extends to the instructor, leader, or facilitator. When I have personal trust, I trust that others will be honest; value my point of view; honor our agreements; respect confidentiality; and provide fair, constructive comments to me.

Strategic Trust

Strategic trust refers to the trust students have in the *strategy* that underpins the learning activity and in the instructor's ability to facilitate it. This includes trust in the fairness and appropriateness of the instructor's strategy for designing a realistic, doable assignment, providing support to students throughout, and assessing the deliverables. Within this category, situational trust more specifically describes making a decision to trust based on characteristics of the situation (Cheng, Nolan, & Macaulay, 2013). When the same characteristics are in place, the student knows she can trust others in a new situation. As a student, once I have had a fair, engaging collaborative learning experience, when another instructor assigns a collaborative activity and creates a situation that requires me to work with others, I trust that I can succeed. I trust that the instructor is using an appropriate pedagogical strategy and the right decisions were made.

Organizational Trust

In an educational context, *organizational trust* refers to the trust students have in larger institutional and curricular systems. The student trusts that there are checks and balances and people beyond the classroom who can provide help if an instructor is unfair or assignments are unrealistic. As a student, I trust that my college, academic program, or course enacted requirements for collaborative learning because they believe this is important to my education. Importantly, I trust that there are appeal protocols available if things go horribly wrong.

If, as instructors or designers, we understand the need for these kinds of trust, we can take steps to communicate the strategic reasons for including collaborative assignments and inform students of the ways to obtain help. We can plan assignments with trust-building activities and time for students to get acquainted before being expected to produce some deliverables. (For more on assignment design, see chapter 5.)

Trust and Safety

When I interviewed educators and students about collaborative learning experiences from both sides of the desk, I was surprised to hear the word *safety* used again and again. Participants intentionally conflated trust and safety when identifying success factors in collaborative e-learning. Research participants described a safe learning environment as one where students trust that others will treat them fairly and respectfully. They consistently pointed out that the instructor has an important role in creating an atmosphere of safety and trust. A similar finding was made by Levesque, Calhoun, Bell, and Johnson (2017); that is, when individuals engaged in social learning feel they can express concerns in a safe environment, they are able to participate more constructively.

Vangen and Huxham (2012) suggest that trust-building must be seen as a cyclic process in which positive outcomes form the basis for deeper trust, enabling more significant levels of collaboration. Their research shows that participants can move forward with a collaborative process even when the partners are getting started and have not yet developed high levels of trust. Adapting their trust-building loop for an educational context, we have two interrelated options as outlined in the following paragraphs.

First, we build on a foundation of strategic or organizational trust. This includes our own credibility and professional reputations. We insist on specific and equitable agreements and articulate norms for acting responsibly. As instructors we are responsible for building strategic trust by communicating fair and realistic expectations, creating assignments that are achievable with learners' given skill levels, and being responsive to concerns. So, while a student may not have yet established trust in the particular peers with whom they are collaborating, they trust that the process is fair and the instructor is there to help if things don't work out.

Second, begin with a small project that encourages collaborative partners to take the risk and initiate collaboration. In my own research, subjects discussed ways to begin with safe, fun, nongraded activities to build learners' confidence and trust. Another small project can be the work agreement itself, which gives them a tangible statement of how they will proceed with the assignment/task they must accomplish collaboratively and how they will be accountable to each other. (See chapter 5 for more on assignments and agreements.)

By understanding the kinds of needs and perspectives students might bring to the learning activity and potential obstacles that might slow down or damage the collaborative process, we can better design and plan an instructional approach. Clearly, instructors cannot compel students to act respectfully and contribute to collaborative efforts with their partners. Students have to assume roles and uphold responsibilities within the collaborative process. Roles and expectations should be clearly defined and agreed on by all parties. By working through decision-making and problem-solving processes, students learn how to build the trust needed to complete work collaboratively. Even so, we typically have time constraints and must prioritize how much time to allocate for acquiring process skills versus for achieving mastery of the course subject matter and learning objectives. Instructors or instructional designers who plan learning activities, assignments, and/or projects need to think through ways to make the best use of students' time.

The *Oxford English Dictionary* defines *dialogue* as "a discussion between two or more people or groups, especially one directed towards exploration of a particular subject or resolution of a problem" (Soanes & Stevenson, 2004, p. 395). This definition is appropriate in the context of collaborative learning. Dialogue is more than communicating; it is directed toward developing a deeper understanding of the subject at hand and resolving the problems or requirements associated with the collaborative learning activity. Dialogue is infused throughout the taxonomy of collaboration. It is fair to say that without communication no collaboration can be successful—on- or offline.

The term *dialogue* is used purposefully here to describe the kind of communication that is characterized by respectful active listening and mutual exchange. The term *conversation* signifies a more informal and less goal-oriented exchange than one characterized by the term *dialogue*. Dialogue, then, is distinguished from the common conversation by the nature of and rationale for the interaction. In dialogue people delve into the subject at hand to find deeper meanings or concepts that can be applied to the solution of a problem. *Dialogue* by the definition used here encompasses the more informal exchanges inferred by the term *conversation*. Brookfield and Preskill (2005) choose to meld the concepts of dialogue and conversation into their definition of *discussion* as a term that incorporates "reciprocity and movement, exchange and inquiry . . . formality and informality" (p. 6). For our purposes—a focus on communication that occurs in the context of the collaborative process—we will retain the distinction and use *dialogue* to refer to communications associated with the formal work of planning, organizing, coordinating, and managing the collaboration. *Conversation* refers to communications associated with the informal exchange needed to build rapport and working relationships. Indeed, the trust and relationship-building associated with casual interchanges may be essential to the deeper and more productive communication we refer to here as *dialogue*.

In an instructional context, dialogue includes discussion between the instructor and the students and among the students engaged in a collaborative project. In community-oriented collaborative projects, students might also need to dialogue with people outside the class. Dialogic teaching draws from Socrates and Plato, who encouraged active learning through self-examination, intelligent dialogue, and interactive communication (Reid, 1998). Social constructivists' perspective on social learning is rooted in a belief that a "reciprocal flow of ideas involving actions and reactions of group members may lead to new understandings not held by any group member in advance of the discussion" (Billings & Fitzgerald, 2002, p. 209). Dialogue is concerned with the development of knowledge, understanding, or judgment. Participants engage in deliberative dialogue that is distinct from other kinds of communication because the intention is not so much to talk together as to think together. When students think together as collaborative partners, they develop a sense of affiliation, affinity, and identity with the group. Hardy highlights the importance of a discursively constructed collective identity. A collective identity "names" the group and allows participants to "construct themselves, the problem, and the solution as part of the collaborative framework in which the potential for joint action is both significant and beneficial" (Hardy et al., 2005, p. 63). She theorizes that once collaborative partners move from "I" to "we," collective identity is translated into "synergistic and innovative action" (p. 59). Hardy and colleagues (2005) point to two kinds of constructions that are defined in a collaboration: common constructions negotiated and agreed upon with partners and private constructions that allow individuals to make sense of and express issues in their own terms. Dialogue with collaborative partners, others in the class, and the instructor are thus complemented by individual reflection and sense-making.

"It all begins with dialogue," states Ram Charan (2001), who believes dialogue "encourages incisiveness and creativity and brings coherence to seemingly fragmented and unrelated ideas" (p. 2). Dialogue is critical at the beginning of a collaborative process, when collaborative partners create a sense of collective identity and purpose, before they take practical steps as needed to work together (Hardy et al., 2005). Dialogue is essential throughout the collaboration when individual and group inputs need to be aligned, quality standards met, and goals revisited. Indeed, through dialogue, collaborative partners build trust and relationships needed to work together and fuse pieces together into a completed project that accomplishes shared goals.

Dialogue is important when disparate contributions are combined into a collective outcome at the culmination of a collaborative project. To create collective outcomes comprising multiple inputs, collaborative partners must be able to look critically at each other's contributions. They must be able to discern which pieces fit and which are extraneous, which ones need to be revised, and what changes must be made, when, and how. These are the kinds of activities described in the taxonomy of collaboration as review. In this context the term *review* is used to describe a process of respectful, constructive mutual critique and feedback between collaborative partners.

Through dialogue, students can learn to do the following:

- Use interpersonal skills and respect others' perspectives.
- Make sure all partners understand elements of the project.
- Determine work design.
- Divide and allocate tasks.
- Establish time lines and standards.
- Coordinate efforts.
- Communicate progress.
- Develop mutual accountability.
- Deal with underperforming participants or resolve conflicts.
- Summarize key points that support the goal of the activity.
- Make decisions in a group.

Dialogue also allows participants to develop and use ICT competencies, such as the following:

- Use synchronous or asynchronous online discussion or conferencing tools to communicate online.
- Participate in or facilitate online discussions.
- Maintain focus on topic.
- Access relevant information and share it with the group using shared folders or other tools.

The second process in the taxonomy of collaboration is *review*. This term is used to describe a process of mutual critique and feedback between learners. Like dialogue, review cannot stand alone and is instead infused throughout the collaborative process. When review is structured with mutually acceptable boundaries and set criteria, learners can provide objective perspectives and learn from each other. Review is particularly important for collaborative work designs that involve both individual and group work. When individuals complete some component of a larger project, others in the group need to look carefully to see whether this element meets agreed-on criteria. They need to determine whether revisions are needed, or stylistic or editorial changes made, for the pieces to be combined into a deliverable that represents the entire group's efforts. Evaluating, selecting, editing, and compiling elements into a collective outcome presupposes skills in constructive criticism practiced and demonstrated in the part of the process we call review.

When two people collaborate, they often must justify their actions to each other, and this is also part of the review dynamic. The verbalization of this knowledge seems to have an effect on both partners. A mechanism observed by sociocultural researchers is termed *appropriation*. Dillenbourg and Schneider (1995) describe it thus:

> Let us consider two agents A and B such as B is more skilled on the task to be performed. When one agent A has performed some action, his or her partner B attempts to integrate A's action into his own plan, i.e., to appropriate A's action. Learning occurs when A reinterprets his actions with respect to how B appropriated it. Agent A learns progressively how to assemble the elementary piece of actions that he is able to perform into a coherent problem strategy. (p. 136)

Vygotsky (1962, 1978) suggested that students learn from a "more knowledgeable other" (Vygotsky, 1978, p. 86); the principle of appropriation suggests that the other also learns. Appropriation aligns with knowledge transfer, as described in the collaborative knowledge model.

Another principle related to the review process is termed *shared cognitive load* by sociocultural researchers. Researchers found that when two subjects collaborate, they often share the cognitive burden inherent in the task and distribute the cognitive subtasks by interest or skill. In some examples, one subject performed low-level operations while the other monitored his or her activities (Miyake, 1986). Palincsar and Brown (1984) and Palincsar and Herrenkohl (2002) observed the reciprocal teaching method in which members of the group take turns as teacher and learner. Johnson and Johnson (1996) also looked at reciprocity and social interdependence. They found that

> where people work in relationships in which each individual depends upon others within the group . . . they achieve more individually, they make greater effort to achieve, they experience greater social support, and they report feelings of greater self-esteem than they do in individualistic and competitive work environments. (p. 5)

Johnson and Johnson (1996) suggest that individuals depend on peer feedback and, when feedback is offered constructively, students perceive the review process as social support. They identified the following review behaviors as essential to successful collaborative learning:

- giving and receiving help and assistance
- challenging others' contributions
- advocating increased effort and perseverance among peers
- monitoring each other's efforts and contributions

Therefore, the placement of review as a central process in the taxonomy of collaboration seems appropriate.

Learning From Experience

In my own teaching experience, the review process was initially intimidating for students. The two most important factors for making it work successfully were creating parameters for the kinds of comments that could be made and making sure students were aware that they could contact me when problems emerged, such as late or inadequate reviews by collaborative partners. Review activities reported by research participants included a lower pressure warm-up activity in an online discussion forum. Students were asked to read each other's work and either make comments or post a summary of key points. This step allowed the instructor to make suggestions or give pointers about ways to give constructive, respectful feedback to another learner. Other examples of preproject review practice included the formal exchange of written assignments for review.

Another research participant encouraged review activities in the context of a buddy system, in which experienced mentors are linked with new learners to teach leadership coaching skills. Peers practiced these skills before they were expected to offer critical comments and feedback to each other.

Learning to review each other's work is part of learning to collaborate. Modeling constructive but critical feedback and offering opportunities to practice allows students to build the confidence they will need to incorporate informal and formal review activities into their collaborative projects. Gillies (2017) points to the importance of teaching students to engage critically and constructively with each other's ideas, challenge perspectives, and discuss alternative propositions. Bloom's original and revised taxonomies placed analysis and evaluation at the top levels. When students analyze and evaluate each other's work in the context of a collaborative assignment in which all are stakeholders, they are able to develop valuable critical thinking skills.

Through participating in a mutual review, students can learn to do the following:

- Trust others to be respectful.
- Give constructive criticism.
- Compare and contrast own ideas with others.
- Work within agreed boundaries.
- Assess which elements to include in a collaborative project—or which elements need revisions.
- Provide respectful, constructive criticism.
- Work within mutually acceptable boundaries and set criteria.

When review occurs electronically, additional skills are needed such as the ability to:

- Work with attachments, shared folders, and other document exchange tools to enter comments and track changes.
- Organize and integrate information into a classification scheme.

Ways to Communicate Using Technology

Collaborative learning in today's world most likely includes at least some technology-mediated communication. Even when students are studying in the same physical classroom, they are likely to communicate electronically and use digital tools to complete the assignment. Students in all-online classes may never meet face-to-face. Some students will study within a learning management system, a closed online site in which students can access course materials and communicate with one another and the instructor. Others will use various platforms, programs, and applications to facilitate their interactions. Given the ever-changing nature of commercial technologies, for our purpose we will focus on communication features and functions, rather than on a particular brand name. Please use these ideas and principles to select the most appropriate technologies or to make the best use of the technologies provided by your institution. It is useful to step back from familiar names for proprietary platforms and analyze the real communication needs, then match the tool to the job (see Figure 3.1 and Table 3.1).

When activities associated with collaborative learning occur online, additional considerations are needed depending on whether communication is carried out using synchronous or asynchronous ICTs. At the simplest, *synchronous communication* refers to real-time, simultaneous communication, and *asynchronous communication* refers to communication that can take place any time. Each form has advantages and disadvantages, and each is appropriate in different situations. Collaborative learning or e-learning can utilize either or both forms.

Synchronous communications occur when everyone is connected at the same time. Web conferencing online meeting platforms allow for robust exchange that is ideal for collaborative partners. These platforms allow you to share screens and video cameras, take notes in a chat area, and share files. Remote students can build rapport and trust and share work in progress. Videoconferencing or video chats focus primarily on the audio and visual exchange; however, these platforms increasingly incorporate web meeting

Figure 3.1. ICTs for collaborative learning.

Information and Communications Features and Platforms for Collaborative Learning	
Text-Based Communicating primarily through typed words in one-on-one or single-group messages or posts. This can also include sharing links, images, or media.	**Social Networking Sites** Communicating with written or visual communications in one-to-one or one-to-many messages or posts. Users can create member-only groups of partners.
Web Conference Communicating through audio, video, text, slides, and/or shared screens or applications.	**Videoconference** Communicating through audio and video. Features can also include text messaging and file sharing.

TABLE 3.1

ICT Features for Synchronous or Asynchronous Dialogue

	Shared Content	*Asynchronous Tools for Dialogue*	*Synchronous Tools for Dialogue*
One-to-One Private exchange between individuals	Secure pages in a learning management system File-sharing in password-protected folders	Private e-mail Comments or track change features on documents	Telephone call Video call or videoconference Text/chat Chat, shared whiteboard, or other features in web or videoconference meeting space
One-to-Many One communicates same message to the group	Content posted on learning management system, web pages, or blogs Podcast/vodcast	E-mail/message list Information or question posted to threaded discussion/bulletin board on social networking site	Webcast or webinar
Many-to-Many Group members communicate with each other without singling out individual recipients	Wiki	Comments or responses made to threaded discussion/bulletin board or comment wall	Conference call Chat, shared whiteboard, or other features in multichannel meeting space Videoconference
Many-to-One Group or members communicate with an individual recipient	Digital assignment drop box for submissions		

Note. This table maps the source-to-audience relationship to types of communications available in online classes. It shows which specific tools might be used for a given combination.

features that allow for screen sharing. Both technologies are synchronous, but meetings can be recorded if someone is unavailable or if the instructor would like evidence of the meeting. Advantages include immediacy and the potential for spontaneity. Decisions can be made without time-consuming back-and-forth messaging. Partners can be assured that everyone has agreed to a decision and can resolve it if they have not. The challenges of synchronous communication include the need for coordination and scheduling. Students must be in the same or close time zones; highly dispersed or international groups are difficult to convene within typical class or business hours.

Text messaging and chatting are also synchronous, but they have the potential for lag time between post and response. I use the term *near-synchronous* to describe these types of exchanges (Salmons, 2016). Social networking sites are primarily asynchronous but may also include near-synchronous features. Some social networking sites allow for closed groups that can be used for collaborative activities.

Asynchronous communications occur at any time. Asynchronous communication requires no scheduling because not all participants need to be connected at the same time. Participants tend to take more time considering what others have posted and to write longer responses compared with written synchronous communications like chat or messaging. The difference is comparable to that between a telephone conversation (synchronous) and written correspondence (asynchronous). Asynchronous communication has applications for education—indeed, forum discussions are common in any learning management system. Discussion occurs in an orderly, linear fashion, so topic drift is less of a problem. Longer posts are possible, as are attachments. Although responses are not spontaneous, they are visible to all and are an important way students contribute to the learning of all in a class.

While it lacks the spontaneity of real-time communication, asynchronous communication is flexible and allows participants to interact despite time or geographic differences. While some products may use a graphic user interface, typically learning management systems, wikis, online community discussion forums, and e-mails are primarily text-based and therefore more accessible to people without broadband connections, an issue to consider when working with students in some rural or international locations.

Another type of technology useful for collaborative partners is less about communication and more about shared resources. These are the shared folders accessible online. As with all these technologies, numerous proprietary platforms exist, and they all operate slightly differently.

Be Present to Support a Collaborative Classroom

The community of inquiry framework (see chapter 2), developed for e-learning, offers some relevant concepts for instructors who want students to feel safe and motivated about collaborating with others—online and offline. To teach in a way that builds a true community of inquiry that supports the development of skills essential for collaboration, instructors need to demonstrate a greater degree of social presence. If the class is offered online, nonverbal cues are absent, which makes addressing this need even more critical. An aspect of online communications relevant to the collaborative process is transactional distance. The term *transactional distance* describes the gap in time between comment and response when interactions occur asynchronously. When multimedia synchronous meeting tools or a hybrid model allow for periodic face-to-face meetings, problems with isolation and transactional distance may decrease.

Garrison (2017) suggests that social presence helps to bridge such gaps and contributes to open communication and group cohesion—two important features of a collaboration-friendly classroom. *Social presence* is defined as the ability to identify with the group, communicate openly in a trusting environment, and develop personal relationships (Garrison, Anderson, & Archer, 2010). Instructors demonstrate social presence to make sure learners are engaged in the interactive process. Garrison (2017) distinguishes social presence in an instructional context from the kinds of interactions we might have in other settings, because the purpose is to support the achievement of academic goals.

Teaching in a way that builds social presence means we are particularly attentive to the ways in which we walk our talk. If we want students to trust each other, we need to show that they can trust us. That means we are conscious of personal levels of trust. We do what we say we will do, follow through, and honor our commitments. We also want to engender confidence at the level of strategic trust by fully explaining the rationale for the collaborative assignment. This rationale might include the significance of the skills they will develop for future academic and professional work in our field. If we want students to be able to communicate with us about concerns before they grow into crises, then we need to be clear about how and when we are available to talk or respond to online messages. We also need to make sure our grading system is aligned with our intentions and avoid penalizing students for revealing problems.

Communication with individual student members of a collaborative project group builds active engagement and instructor–student trust. Individual interactions can include comments on reflective journals, meetings, or e-mail communication. These communications are most effective when you use a positive tone and personal language and affirm successful aspects of learners' work. Group comments—those made to the class as a whole or to the collaborative project group—should aim to create a welcoming learning community and model respectful behaviors that are essential to successful collaboration. Collective interaction builds community and student–student trust. Discussion with the class as a whole is an opportunity to show how learners' work builds on and complements each other's ideas. Feedback to the group can take the form of comments on their agreements and reports, small-group meetings, or group e-mail. In both cases, give constructive feedback with specific suggestions. (See chapters 5 and 6 for more on instructional strategies and formative assessment.)

In my own experience, offering a friendly introduction at the very beginning of the class helped to set the tone. I tried to convey a "we are in this together" message. I discussed my own experiences in relation to the types of subject matter and assignments in an effort to build credibility and strategic trust. In a face-to-face class, that could be accomplished with a warm introduction and an icebreaker that encourages everyone to get acquainted. In an online class, a similar approach can be used. I offered a synchronous web meeting, using my web camera, so students could see me and be assured that someone was present on the other side of the monitor. Throughout the term I created short recordings and posted them in the learning management system to keep students motivated and provide suggestions about how to overcome obstacles they might be facing. I found that the use of audio or audiovisual tools helped to convey a sense of warmth and encouragement. Ask your students for input at the end of the term—not just the usual course evaluation form. What approaches helped them stay on track and feel confident about learning collaboratively? As with any change in instructional strategy, the first term might require some extra time and effort. However, once you find your own style for facilitating collaborative learning, you might discover, as I did, that it does not require an increased workload.

Key Questions: Prompts for Discussion or Reflection

Reflect on your most recent experience with collaboration or teamwork.

- Would you characterize your feelings about the project and those involved as exemplifying personal, strategic, or organizational trust? Why or why not?
- If you have experienced successful personal trust in an academic setting, describe what the individual did to gain your trust. Did that

person also provide a sense of social presence in their interactions? If so, describe the online or face-to-face approaches you deem successful.

- How did you communicate with other members of the collaborative project group? What worked or didn't work? What would you do to communicate more effectively? Did you communicate electronically? If so, what tools or platforms worked best and why?
- In your collaborative or team experience, did one or more members of the group review or critique your work? What did the reviewer do to build or obstruct confidence in the process? How could you use what you've learned to teach others how to provide constructive criticism to peers?

4

COLLABORATIVE WORK DESIGNS

Coming together is a beginning; keeping together is progress; working together is success.

—Henry Ford

Objectives

Chapter 4 will prepare you to:

- Differentiate between collaborative work design options.
- Analyze learning potential for assignments using one or more collaborative work designs.
- Know the importance of infusing dialogue and review processes into collaborative work designs.

Introduction

The concept of work design suggests that collaborative partners need to make strategic decisions about how they organize the work. In chapter 4 we will use the taxonomy of collaboration in conjunction with other theories and models to explore collaborative work design. These principles can be applied to any kind of professional or community work, but for the purpose of this book, they are applied to teaching and learning. We will look at ways students can work together to plan and complete simple learning activities or complex projects. Chapter 5 is dedicated to more specific steps you can take to design assignments that fit with your workshop, seminar, or course. Chapter 5 also includes discussion of the types of agreements collaborative partners should make before beginning work on an assignment. Chapter 6 focuses on the types of assessment that can be used to formalize feedback and determine performance as needed to provide grades or completion certificates.

A fundamental decision necessary when we are planning to work together is: Who does what? Broadly speaking, we have two options. The first option is to divide a large undertaking into parts that can be completed by individuals or small groups. The second option is to work in a holistic way and complete the entire effort together. One is not better than the other; the important thing is to align the work design with the purpose and other relevant factors. The taxonomy of collaboration offers three types of collaborative work designs. Two of these designs, parallel and sequential, use the first option; that is, they involve completion of discrete parts of a larger effort. The third design, synergistic, depends on the second option, in which everyone works together. These types of collaborative work can be used individually or combined, depending on the type and scope of the assignment.

The attitudes, efforts, and protocols associated with dialogue and review are essential with all these options. To divide the large undertaking into parts that can be completed separately, we will need to discuss the project and think it through very carefully to determine how it can be segmented. We will typically need to combine those elements into one deliverable. To do so, we need to respectfully discuss and review the elements we completed on our own. We will need to communicate and make decisions to inductively create a coherent whole from these parts.

Depending on the characteristics of the students and the nature of the assignment, the collaborative knowledge learning model (see chapter 1) advances the collaborative activities involved with these work designs.

- *Knowledge exchange*, sharing information or resources, is essential throughout the various steps involved with collaborative learning.
- *Knowledge transfer*, learning from a knowledgeable or experienced partner, can occur during learning activities associated with dialogue, review, and collaboration. These learning activities can complement individual work completed through parallel or sequential work designs.
- *Knowledge acquisition*, learning new concepts or skills together, can occur during learning activities associated with dialogue, review, and synergistic collaboration. These learning activities can complement individual work completed through parallel or sequential work designs.
- *Knowledge cocreation*, generating new knowledge, solutions, or practices, can be the outcome of synergistic collaboration or can be the result of the whole collaborative learning assignment.

Bloom's taxonomy of cognitive processes and knowledge types can also be useful when describing collaborative learning activities. What kinds of knowledge are our students exchanging, transferring, acquiring, and/or cocreating in the collaborative assignment? Does the assignment focus on factual, conceptual, procedural, or metacognitive knowledge? Students can work together to remember and understand the foundations of curricular material. Students participating in service-learning or internship placements might collaborate in the application of skills and knowledge needed to provide a needed service. Students involved with projects that aim for knowledge cocreation collaborate when they create new solutions or strategies.

Opportunities and Challenges With Collaborative Work Designs

Parallel work designs are probably the most common way individuals work together. The *Oxford English Dictionary* defines *in parallel* as "taking place at the same time and having some connection" (Soanes & Stevenson, 2004, p. 1038). In our context, the "same time" will refer to the same time frame. Students can work synchronously or asynchronously to complete their individual tasks. Tasks are connected as part of the same assigned learning activity or project and are intended to meet the shared goals set by the instructor or the group. When parallel collaboration is used, tasks are allocated among participants. Through parallel work designs students can learn to do the following:

- Determine and achieve a shared goal or purpose.
- Develop protocols in terms of timing, coordination, communication styles, and other expectations.
- Create agreements for how they will combine individual contributions into the collective outcome.
- Develop mutual accountability.
- Deal with underperforming team members and resolve conflicts.
- Generate new knowledge by adapting and synthesizing multiple perspectives into a collective whole.

Dialogue processes are critical to parallel collaboration because to allocate tasks, the group members first need to fully understand the assignment as a whole. What are we being asked to do? What are the deliverables? Are there deliverables we are expected to develop as individuals? How will we know that the pieces created by individuals will be of comparable style and quality to combine them? Which of those deliverables are we expected to develop as a group?

Depending on the size of the work group, these tasks could be divided among individuals or smaller subgroups. Whether in a face-to-face or virtual environment, tasks are completed side-by-side. This means there are minimal dependencies between these discrete tasks. In other words, I can fulfill my part of the work without waiting for you to complete your part. If the group members determine that there are dependencies or that steps need to build progressively, they might decide to use a sequential approach instead of a parallel one.

Another decision the group needs to make relates to the criteria individuals will use to determine whether they are on track with their tasks. Criteria could be provided by the instructor as part of the assignment or as part of an assessment rubric. (See chapter 6 for more about assessment and rubrics.) Group members might want to add other criteria about the quality they expect from one another, as well as the timing for completion of each part. Group members might add other mutual expectations, such as frequency of communication while the tasks are underway. Practical decisions, such as what platforms or shared folders to use, should be made at the outset of the assignment. Protocols for formatting and writing style are important for written assignments. Protocols for design, file type, and length are important for audio or media. Coordination of these efforts takes time and effort—typically characteristics associated with the dialogue stage of the taxonomy.

If students are combining component parts into one deliverable, additional stages will be needed. In a review process, students will look at and critique each other's work to determine whether refinements and revisions are needed so they fit together. Further dialogue will be needed as they discuss how to put the pieces together. They might find that they need to work synergistically at this stage. After students have completed individual components, knowledge cocreation can occur when they combine these parts into assignment deliverables.

Trust is needed among the group members throughout the planning, decision-making, and work stages. (See chapter 3 for more about the trust collaborative process.) Members need to trust each other's commitment to fairness when allocating tasks to be completed in parallel. They need to trust that others are doing their part during times when they are working independently. They need to trust fellow group members who review their work: Was the review respectful and constructive? Trust also helps to facilitate learning the subject matter content associated with the assignment and course. Knowledge exchange, knowledge transfer, and knowledge acquisition can occur in the dialogue activities that take place throughout the assignment. If there are what Vygotsky (1978) calls *knowledgeable others*, they can transfer what they know to others in the group.

Apply the Ideas

Let's look at how these points might fit together in assignments and map the processes. (See chapter 5 for more on the design of collaborative assignments and optional rules for instructors.) Using the same assignment example, we can compare and contrast how students might complete it using parallel, sequential, or synergistic work designs together with dialogue and review processes. For this assignment exemplar, students are asked to collaboratively create a poster or slide presentation that references at least six sources and offers a set of recommendations for future research. Each student is asked to submit an annotated bibliography of the articles he or she consulted for the project. This assignment has a collective deliverable created by the group (the presentation) and an individual deliverable (annotated bibliography). The instructor divides the class into groups of three students, or students self-select collaborative partners.

Students who complete the assignment using parallel design for part of the work will need to begin with a discussion and planning session (see Figure 4.1). Once the parts of the work that can be completed in parallel are ready, students need to think about how they will mesh these elements into the final presentation. This assignment also has an individual component with an individual deliverable. By including expectations for the individuals

Figure 4.1. Assignment with a parallel design focus.

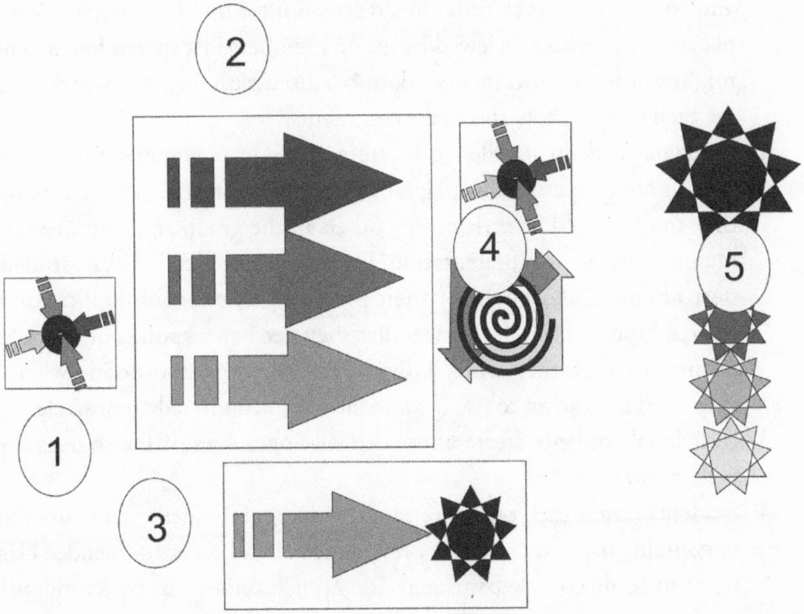

in the group, the instructor and fellow group members can instill mutual accountability.

1. In the first meeting, the students discuss the assignment and agree to a plan. How many parts make up this assignment? Can they be evenly divided? What do we need to establish in terms of a common format for presentation slides, graphics, or text? When will each part need to be completed to have enough time to combine them into the final presentation? Using dialogue approaches, they discuss the assignment and divide up responsibilities. For the purpose of this example they decide that each student should contribute four slides with key points drawn from at least two sources.

   In an online or blended class, students could use a web conferencing platform or conference call for this important initial discussion. At the outset, online students need to decide what communication tools they would like to use for this project. Their plan and work agreement could be posted in the learning management system discussion forum. If they are not interacting in a formal course that uses a learning management system, they might want to use a wiki or a blogging platform that allows them to create members-only places to share documents and make comments. To what extent do they want to work synchronously or asynchronously? Do they prefer to use e-mail or to post work in progress and comments to each other in a discussion forum? They might want to place all the articles reviewed by group members in a shared folder. They might want to upload their work into a discussion forum where they can see each others' posts and make comments.
2. Students work in parallel to locate and study potential sources. They make note of quotations, diagrams, examples, or other key points that they think should be reviewed by others in the group and considered for inclusion in the final presentation. In an online or blended class, students post resources and notes for their peers to see, to avoid duplication of efforts. Students can decide whether they need checkpoints or check-ins during the time they work individually. They can also decide whether they need a protocol to use if someone has encountered an obstacle.
3. Individual students create annotated bibliographies of the sources they have reviewed.
4. Students review each others' research findings and slides and discuss ways to combine them to create the presentation. In an online or blended class, students could complete this step either synchronously or asynchronously.

5. Students make a presentation to peers in the class and submit slides. Students submit annotated bibliographies. In an online or blended class, students could record the presentation and post a link where the instructor and other students in the class can view it.

In summary, parallel work designs allow for efficient completion of assignments that have multiple parts or sections. However, working in parallel cannot succeed without dialogue and review. While the main work is completed in parallel, without the initial dialogue or the review process, group members could not deliver a coherent presentation. The addition of the individual assignment adds accountability for each student's participation.

Sequential Collaboration

Another way to organize a collaborative process is through a sequential work design (see Figure 4.2). When a group uses a sequential structure to complete a project, components of the project are organized into a series of progressive steps. Each component is dependent on successful completion of the previous step. Each step may involve individual as well as collective work by a subgroup. Participants determine how each contribution is integrated into the final product through a process of dialogue and review. In addition to the competencies for coordination, quality control, and accountability in parallel designs, through sequential collaboration, students can learn the following:

Figure 4.2. Assignment with a sequential design focus.

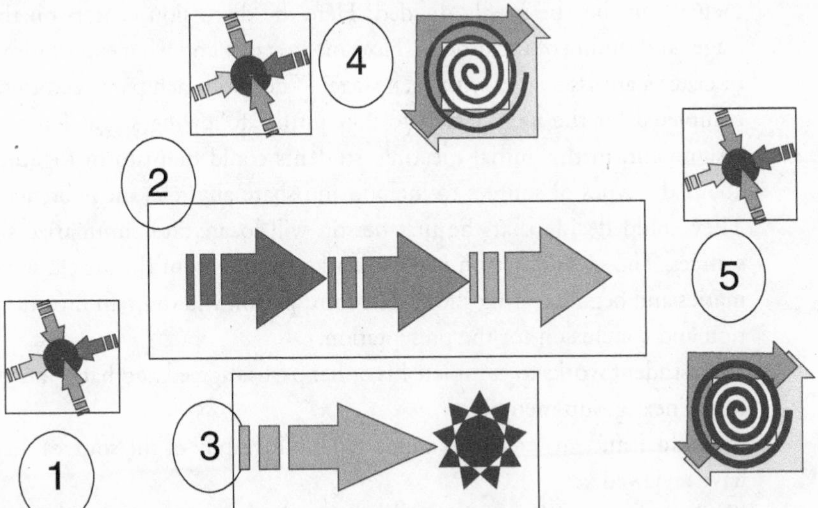

- Coordinate timing and multistep processes.
- Use quality control criteria to assess deliverables at each stage.
- Engage members from all stages in creation of a collective outcome.

In addition to the ICT tools described for parallel designs, students can learn the following:

- Use project management tools to track progress.
- Use advanced editing and version control software functions.

With the use of sequential designs, a greater degree of trust is needed among the group members. In addition to points made in the description of parallel designs, the coordination needed for sequential work requires clear mutual respect. Members need to trust that others responsible for earlier parts will complete them on time. Each part needs to be completed with sufficient quality to build the next stage upon it. Trust also helps to facilitate learning the subject matter content associated with the assignment and course.

Many of the issues related to analyzing the assignment and clarifying the format and style of presentation, using online tools to support communication and review, are the same. Let's see how the characteristics unique to the sequential style play out, using the same assignment as the one used in the parallel work design example.

1. Similar to the parallel process, in the first meeting, the students discuss the assignment and agree to a plan. How many parts make up this assignment? Can they be evenly divided? Here the discussion centers on the stages and timing of the process. How many stages and what expectations or criteria are associated with each stage? When will each part need to be completed for the next person to take up the following stage? For this assignment, in this initial meeting, students could brainstorm together about the types of sources to include and share any relevant references. They could decide that the first person will locate and summarize six sources. The second person will extract key points from the article summaries and begin creating slides. The third person will draft an introduction and conclusion for the presentation.
2. Each student works to complete his or her part as agreed and hand it over to the next group member.
3. Individual students create an annotated bibliography of the sources they have reviewed.
4. While the sequential process is underway, students may decide they need to discuss the work in progress or review the parts of the project in development.

5. Group members review and discuss the completed parts and combine them to create the presentation. Individual and collective deliverables are submitted.

Synergistic

The third way people design work to be completed together is through synergistic collaboration. When a group uses a synergistic structure, the students synthesize their ideas and work through all stages of the project to plan, organize, and complete the project together. Their contributions are fully melded into the collective final product (see Figure 4.3).

Unlike the parallel and sequential work designs, those working synergistically do not divide up the assignment. While individuals may need to conduct research or complete readings to prepare, the primary activities are carried out together. In a teaching and learning context, when the assignment is divided up, it is simpler for the instructor to see the contributions of individuals. In the synergistic collaboration, individual contributions are transformed through the interaction with other collaborative partners. This means collaborative partners typically need a review stage during which individuals' contributions are considered, potentially revised, then combined

Figure 4.3. Assignment with a synergistic design focus.

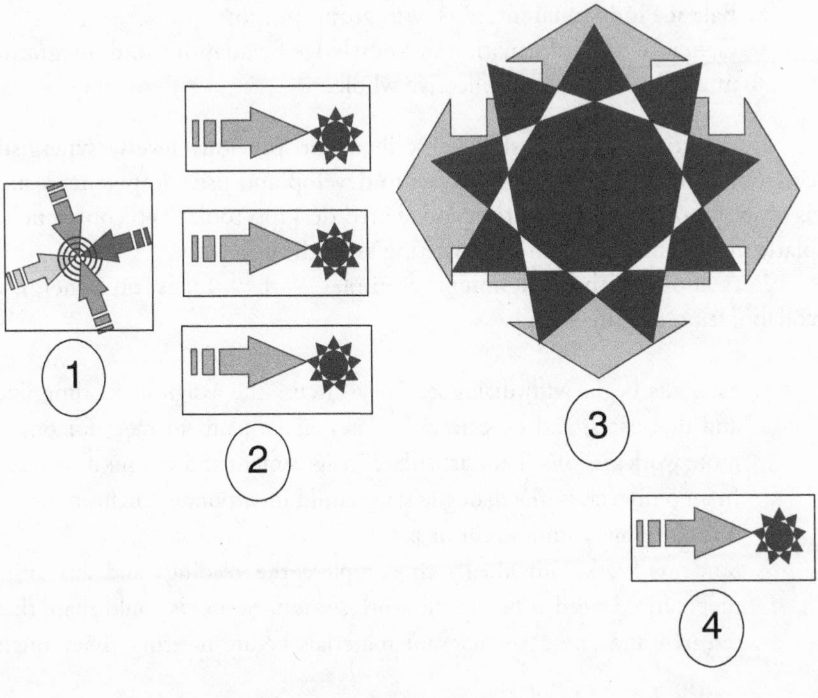

into a collective outcome. In a synergistic process, there are no separate parts to combine; the collaborative partners generate the deliverable as an ensemble. This type of collaboration may incorporate all levels of the collaborative knowledge learning model but is uniquely poised for knowledge cocreation. Partners do more than discuss what to do; they think together about how to do it (London, 2005).

A higher level of trust is needed because collaborative partners need to feel confident in each other to share ideas and surrender an individual perspective into a group perspective. In this type of collaboration, partners move from a sense of "I" to an identity as "we." Hardy and colleagues (2005) describe this transition as producing collective identity, which enables participants to construct themselves, the problem, and the solution as part of a collaborative framework in which the potential for joint action is both significant and beneficial.

Synergistic collaboration depends on synchronous interactions, whether in person or online. Coordination and commitment are essential. In addition to the group process and digital literacy competencies described previously, through synergistic collaboration, students can learn to do the following:

- Interact with group members at all stages of project.
- Practice participatory decision-making.
- Balance individual interests with group purpose.
- Generate new information or knowledge by adapting and integrating multiple parts into a collective whole.

In addition to ICT skills described for previous levels, synergistic collaboration also allows participants to develop and use competencies such as synchronous communication and shared desktop tools, web conferencing platforms for meetings, and live writing and editing.

Let's look at the assignment exemplar with a focus on synergistic collaboration (Figure 4.3).

1. Students begin with dialogue. They discuss the assignment, time lines and due dates, and expectations. They make plans to meet for one or more work sessions. They articulate an agreement and submit if required. In an online class, the dialogue stage could incorporate synchronous and asynchronous communications.
2. Students work individually to complete the readings and any other preparations needed before the work session. Students could share their research and any other relevant materials before meeting. They might

use shared folders and other tools to save their research and analysis and make it available to collaborative partners.

3. This is the stage in which students meet to analyze and evaluate what they have learned from their readings and preparations. They share ideas and brainstorm solutions, working together to complete assignment requirements and create the presentation.
4. At this stage using what was learned from the collaborative process, students complete their individual annotated bibliographies as required by the assignment.

Applying Collaborative Work Designs

Dialogue and review are inherent to all the collaborative work designs described here. Most of the projects discussed by research participants started with a dialogue stage. Coming to an agreement about how the work will be completed is one purpose for the initial dialogue. Huxham discusses learning about partners and their interest in the outcomes of the collaboration as critical to engagement in the collaborative process (Hibbert & Huxham, 2005). Students who were interviewed after taking the course that I modeled on the taxonomy of collaboration echoed this point: "We made a personal contact to get acquainted and each of the strengths and weaknesses. It was not all about logistics, it was about who we were." Another student commented: "The most important thing was the personal conversation, and knowing I could depend on someone."

Nearly half of the research participants in my study described some kind of individual reflective or written assignment as part of the collaborative activity. In my own teaching experience, the role of the individual within the group could be understood through written assignments that invite students to reflect on their own experience while at the same time discussing related literature. In courses with subject matter unrelated to collaboration, the inclusion of some short, practical readings can help students learn how to collaborate while collaborating to learn. Reflective individual assignments are the "private constructions" that complement the "common constructions" of understandings developed with the group (Hardy et al., 2005, p. 67). Both kinds of construction are important because, when divergent private and common constructions are juxtaposed, creative and innovative outcomes may result.

Parallel and sequential work designs, when combined with effective planning sessions and review processes, allow for a flexible mix of individual and group work. Review exchanges ask students to use criteria to evaluate what they read, then organize and integrate information into a classification scheme provided in the assignment. Parallel and sequential designs usually require students to create their own classification schemes and protocols for organizing, managing, and integrating information from multiple inputs. Activities that expect students to classify and categorize various elements of the assignment subject matter, then summarize and generalize what they've learned, fit within what is called *conceptual knowledge* in the revised Bloom's taxonomy (Anderson et al., 2000).

Students and instructors with little experience in collaboration may find these structured approaches to be more accessible. These ways of organizing work are ideal for hybrid courses in which in-person class time can be used for discussion and for developing deliverables, while individual work and reflection can occur electronically. In an all-online class, synchronous and asynchronous interactions can be used to facilitate communication at various stages of the assignment. Whether students are in an online or a hybrid course, success is dependent on creation of and commitment to a work agreement. (See chapter 5 for more on work agreements.)

Synergistic work designs are hierarchically more sophisticated and require both more skills and a higher degree of trust. Several of the students I interviewed described very systematic plans for using dialogue, review, and sequential stages. They found that this organized approach enabled them to get into a collaborative flow that allowed them to work synergistically at the final stage. One noted, "Trust was built around performance, including fair reviews of each other's work." Another observed, "We wanted [the final assignment] to have the same feel throughout, rather than have separate pieces. At the synergistic stage, all ideas developed individually were accounted for, and new ideas were generated."

Truly synergistic collaboration engages students at all levels of the knowledge dimension. Collaborative partners need to familiarize themselves with factual knowledge to participate. They use procedural knowledge for group decision-making and meeting facilitation. The self-knowledge intrinsic to the metacognitive level is also important because collaborative partners need to know their own abilities and limits when it comes to how they work with others.

Some people find the creative process involved with synergistic designs to be exciting and energizing. As one research participant commented, "It has to do with my worldview. I like to work synergistically, I like working with other people to build ideas, it is part of my value system; it is embedded in who I am." Others, particularly in all-online classes, might find that the need to work primarily in a synchronous manner is burdensome. Instructors in such courses can help students schedule and organize meetings, demonstrate the use of meeting technologies, and include meeting plans in the initial agreement.

Key Questions: Prompts for Discussion or Reflection

Reflect on your most recent experience with collaboration or teamwork.

- How would you categorize the style you used? How did the style or styles fit the taxonomy of collaboration work designs?
- How did you decide what approach you would use to complete the project? Did you decide at the beginning of the project, or did the approach evolve throughout the project?
- Did you come to an agreement, formally or informally, about who would do what?
- What was your role? Who decided what your role was to be? Was it decided by others in the group, by you, or by someone else, such as a supervisor or instructor? How did you feel about your role? Did you feel the work was allocated fairly?
- If you were approaching the same project today, how would you organize it?

PART THREE

PLANNING AND ASSESSING COLLABORATIVE LEARNING

5

DESIGNING COLLABORATIVE LEARNING WITH THE TAXONOMY OF COLLABORATION

Be as collaborative as possible—my philosophy is that learning is increasing peoples' ability and we increase people's abilities by enhancing their networks and neural networks are only one network; social networks can be much more powerful. Effective learning in the future will be less about developing individual capacities and more developing collaborative capacities.

—Research participant

Objectives

Chapter 5 will prepare you to:

- Apply concepts from chapters 1 through 4 in the design of learning activities.
- Plan activities that use an appropriate instructional style.
- Work with students to develop agreements that establish roles and expectations.

Introduction

Bruner's (1997) pre-Internet observations suggest reasons why developing active, problem-based collaborative assignments merit our best efforts.

> The best way to create interest in a subject is to render it worth knowing, which means to make the knowledge gains usable in one's thinking beyond the situation in which the learning has occurred. . . . Knowledge one has acquired without sufficient structure to tie it together is knowledge that is likely to be forgotten. (p. 31)

When learners perceive a subject as "worth knowing" and relevant to their own inquiry, life, and work, they will be engaged in the learning process enough to contribute their own insights. How can we convey that learning how to collaborate, in conjunction with learning the course's subject matter, is worth knowing? In an era when text messaging, social media, e-mail, and blogging are common ways students interact socially, collaborative learning encourages students to apply these practices to meaningful tasks.

Students can benefit from purposeful collaboration, whether the class is taught online, face-to-face, or in a blended combination. To successfully collaborate, people need to agree on fundamental goals and processes. Why and how will we work together? Who will do what? When you are faced with the need to work with a group, where do you start? Do you think about ways to divide up the project into parts that can be completed by individuals or small groups? Will you take a "You do this, I'll do that" approach? Or do you plan a meeting during which everyone contributes to brainstorming ways to address the dilemma? Do you look at stages or timing for getting parts of the project completed? Will you think about what needs to happen first—perhaps doing some background reading or contacting important stakeholders—before the next stage can occur? Will you consider the means you will use to communicate with collaborative partners or think about the need for common technology approaches, such as shared folders and writing tools that allow for multiple comments? When you think about the best way to get things done to meet whatever deadlines or goals must be achieved, do you think about the other members in your group and whether you can count on them to do their parts? Might you fear that someone will try to dominate the process while someone else will disappear at a critical moment and leave you with extra work?

If you have experience with collaborative projects, you probably have some ideas about how you would answer these questions. You'll communicate with your collaborative partners and come to an agreement about ground rules and checkpoints. You'll try to take a proactive approach to ensure that everyone knows what is expected and who to contact if a problem arises. How can we design learning activities that enable students to acquire the skills and confidence they will require when they confront the need to collaborate in later academic or professional life?

In an educational context the answers to some of these fundamental questions, such as goals and desired learning outcomes, may be driven by curricular standards. Others, such as technology choices, may be determined by the information technology infrastructure of the school; the learning management system; or the institution's policies about using free, Internet-based options. In chapter 6, the assumption is that you have the freedom to make the choices you feel are best. As with all the suggestions made in this book, you are invited to take what works for you and adapt recommendations to fit your situation.

Factors to Consider at the Design Stage

Four interrelated factors are important to consider when designing collaborative learning experiences. They include time and focus, student characteristics and instructional roles, setting, and agreements. Based on our evaluation of these factors, we can decide what types of collaborative activities will be beneficial and appropriate to the course or programs.

Time and Focus

Time and focus are interrelated because we first need to decide how much time we can allocate to the activity. The ideas presented in this book could be applied to a one-day workshop, a multisession professional development program, an academic course, or an entire academic program. Decisions are needed at the design stage that depend on the type and length of learning experience. Are we looking for collaborative activity for a single class meeting, an extended project for entire semester, or a longer term project that might continue throughout an academic program?

Within the available time, to what extent do we want students to focus on acquisition of knowledge and skills in the subject matter, and to what extent do we want students to focus on acquisition of knowledge and skills related to the collaborative process? In other words, how will we balance the need to learn to collaborate and the need to collaborate to learn?

This decision is often influenced by the subject matter we are teaching. In some situations, such as a class on leadership or management, the collaborative process might be part of the content. In such cases, we can take more time to discuss and practice related ideas. In other situations, the collaborative process is not directly related to the subject matter of the course, so our choices for organizing collaborative assignments must reflect a different set of priorities. When the curriculum is highly structured and preset, we may have less flexibility about making time for extensive planning for and reflecting on the collaborative experience. One way we can make the most productive use of available time involves careful thought about the degree of structure and the roles the instructor and students will take.

Student Characteristics and Instructional Roles

When we think about ways to use time wisely, we need to answer questions about who does what, when, and how. Many instructors who want to teach collaboratively ask themselves: Which roles and responsibilities should I take, and what should I expect from the students? How much structure, guidance, and direction should I offer, and how much latitude should learners have for self-determination, self-management, and self-efficacy? To what extent should I impose parameters, and to what extent should I allow students to establish their own? One way to think through these options is by considering the instructional style. Three options are shown in Figure 5.1. These options are presented on a continuum to suggest that they are not necessarily firmly differentiated. Some instructors, particularly those who are designing and teaching more extended collaborative projects, may find that they use all these styles at different points.

When using an instructor-driven style, the instructor organizes the collaborative process, assigns group members and roles, provides templates for necessary agreements, and offers clear expectations for the assignment and criteria for assessing outcomes. Parameters for student interactions and for acceptable approaches for completion of the project are spelled out. The instructor might provide lectures or readings about group formation and process. The instructor exercises control by determining the subject matter as well as process-oriented content. If the collaborative assignment is students' first opportunity for meaningful interaction in a learning environment where lectures are common, an instructor-driven approach might offer the framework students need to begin collaborating.

An instructor-driven style may be chosen intentionally as a way to encourage students to try a new and perhaps more challenging approach to collaboration. The instructor may need to guide, help structure, and organize the process so students do not simply operate in the ways they already know, but develop new approaches to respond to increasingly complex challenges. For example, if students are accustomed to working in a simple parallel mode, an instructor-driven approach might offer the support they need to venture into a synergistic mode of collaboration. By using the resources provided by the instructor, students learn about the kinds of topics collaborative partners need to address to lay the foundations for their work together. Students who have experienced this style of collaborative process will be prepared to take more responsibility for the organization and management of future projects.

At the other end of the continuum, with a student-centered mode, collaborative learning occurs with little or no intervention from the instructor—beyond making the assignment. Students are responsible for finding compatible group members, agreeing to the way they work together, and developing a

Figure 5.1. Instructional styles continuum.

Building trust: Roles for instructors and students

Instructor Driven

Instructor provides instructional, cognitive, and social presence in support of the students' collaborative work.

Dialogue: Primarily instructor>student

Instructor is responsible for:

- Assigning the collaborative learning activity or project
- Communicating measurable goals
- Forming student groups
- Creating templates for group agreement, project and time management
- Leading start-up exercises
- Assigning readings and resources
- Monitoring learning activity
- Troubleshooting, coaching students when problems arise

Guided Facilitation

Instructor provides cognitive and social presence in support of the students' collaborative work. Instructional presence is offered when needed.

Dialogue: student>instructor>student

Instructor is responsible for:

- Assigning the collaborative learning activity or project
- Clarifying expectations and parameters
- Supporting students through group formation
- Assigning core readings and pointing students toward other relevant resources
- Facilitating discussions with students on collaborative process or other assignment content
- Offering examples, resources, coaching, and guidance, as needed

Student Driven

Instructor provides social presence in support of the students' collaborative work. Cognitive and instructional presence are offered when needed.

Dialogue: student>student>instructor

Students are responsible for:

- Interpreting assignment requirements, asking questions for clarification
- Forming and organizing the group, including how decisions will be made, and who does what tasks
- Reading assigned materials, doing research to find additional sources

strategy for achieving the assignment. They will craft their own agreement and communicate what they need from the instructor. The focus is on reciprocal peer exchange: content contributed by or generated by the students.

Student-driven collaboration may have some trial and error as students experiment with the collaborative process. For example, they might initially think that working synergistically would be ideal, but, after scheduling problems, shift to another style. Even so, the students have many opportunities to learn about what makes a collaboration successful and will be more confident about taking on complex collaborative projects in the future. They can build camaraderie and a culture of participatory learning. A challenge is that the student groups can lose focus and get distracted by extraneous details. Without the cognitive and instructional presence of the instructor, incorrect information can be perpetuated.

For a hybrid approach, we use guided facilitation. The instructor is present to guide, coach, and support students through the collaborative process. The instructor is available to answer questions or troubleshoot problems that arise. The instructor facilitates discussions with the class as a whole, or the small group, to work through the kinds of decision-making dilemmas collaborative partners face. Guided facilitation allows students to try out leadership and decision-making skills, with the safety of knowing the instructor is there when needed. Both instructor and learners contribute content, and learners may help to determine topics or process. This means there is more interaction and more meaningful interaction among learners and between instructor and learners. This flexible approach works in many situations, but it requires a shared commitment and focus.

Learning How to Collaborate: Balancing Instructor and Student Roles

Finding the appropriate balance between instructor and student roles in collaborative e-learning is the central inquiry at the heart of e-social constructivism and a taxonomy of collaboration system. Time spent learning how to collaborate versus collaborating to learn varies across this continuum. In an instructor-driven situation, students focus more of their time on the subject matter of the assignment, because the organizational side of the collaborative process is developed and structured by the instructor. Time needed to negotiate agreements is reduced because they simply complete the form provided by the instructor. At the other end of the continuum, a student-driven collaborative project will require additional time for students to engage in a dialogue stage because they will need time to determine the roles and stages necessary for completion of the assignment. Additional time is taken whenever a change is needed to refine the agreement or plan. With guided facilitation the instructor can monitor the time being spent and adjust. For example, if a group is getting bogged down in the agreement stage, the instructor can step in and offer recommendations that allow the group to move forward.

In a student-centered curriculum, some collaborations may occur with little or no intervention from the instructor. But given the role of the instructor suggested in chapters 1 and 2—to develop learning experiences that create a bridge between learners' existing knowledge and the next level of knowledge—learner-directed collaborative learning may not be adequate. The instructor may need to guide, help structure, and organize the process so learners do not simply operate in the ways they already know, but develop new approaches to respond to increasingly complex challenges.

The decision about timescales and instructional style also relates to the scope of the assignment. A collaborative learning activity designed to be a part of a single class for a learning unit might be more successful with an instructor-driven approach that allows students to move quickly into the heart of the work, because less planning and communicating is required. The instructor is likely to be present and available to provide additional instruction if students do not understand what is expected or how to proceed.

In a collaborative project designed to be carried out over months or years, a guided facilitation or student-driven approach may be appropriate. For one thing, students would have more time to complete a full, realistic set of steps from group formation through completion. For another, students working over a longer term have greater need for agreements about how they will communicate, make decisions, and solve problems.

My own teaching experience in all online graduate classes has used all three of these styles. I typically formed the groups and selected one student to serve as the leader for the initial stage. In this stage students were responsible for creating a work agreement, which included making decisions about leadership. Beyond the initial meeting, they could use a student-driven approach for the duration of the project. They could choose to have one person serve as a leader throughout the project, to rotate leadership roles, or to operate as a self-managed group without one person identified as a leader. Here is an excerpt from an introductory message explaining student expectations:

> Please go to the team folder and make a post to introduce yourself. Even though the group assignments formally begin in week 2, please use this time to get acquainted and to make sure everyone is able to access the folder. I've asked one member to serve as the first leader, to coordinate efforts on the charter. Part of the charter involves determining your team's leadership for the rest of the term. See the unit overview and the syllabus for more details.

As noted, I allowed time before the start of the project for students to get acquainted—without the pressure of needing to accomplish any formal activities.

Student Characteristics and Student Needs

These options are considered by the instructor depending on the characteristics of the students. Critical questions include: Are the students experienced with group work or teamwork, or is this their first significant collaborative project? Have the students had a chance to build some level of trust in other coursework? If so, they may be ready for a student-driven experience for some or all of the project. What kinds of instruction are common in the educational setting? Are students accustomed to free-flowing discussion and active, problem-based learning? Or are they accustomed to large classes in a lecture hall with little peer interaction? How do we determine students' entry characteristics? I have used a straightforward approach: I asked them. In the first assignment for the course, before the collaborative project was introduced, I posed these questions for a written assignment and discussed these questions as a class.

1. What is your experience with teams or small groups? If you have not worked in a group, discuss your thoughts and feelings about working with your peers on an assignment.
2. What is your experience with virtual group work? If you have had experience, how did you use communications technology? What was effective or ineffective?
3. What roles have you played in group work? What behaviors help and what behaviors hinder group work?
4. What was successful or unsuccessful in your experience with group work? Explain.
5. Is there any specific aspect of the practice of collaboration that you want to explore in more depth?

Another approach is more open-ended and serves as a self-assessment. As such, it can be complemented with an end-of-project self-assessment. (See chapter 6 for more about assessment.)

- When working with a group, I would describe my leadership style as:
- When working with a group, I would describe my collaborative style as:
- My main strengths as a contributor to a group project are:

- When working with groups, I use my strengths in the following ways:
- I can become more effective with groups by:
- Three skills or behaviors I will work on developing in this course:

When students bring a background in team or group work, it's possible that prior collaborative experiences were negative. They may have had bad experiences in other classes or in workplace settings. Here is an excerpt from a message I sent to adult students after a discussion that generated discomfort when they discovered the collaborative project assignment in the syllabus:

> As you have seen from our discussion, some of us have good examples to look to from our work experience, and we can model and build on those successful strategies when we work with others in this class. Some of us do not have those good experiences. We have seen too many examples where command-and-control styles did not align with meaningful collaboration. When we work with others, we have to be on guard lest we repeat those unsuccessful approaches. We will have to develop trust, gain more understanding of effective safeguards, and use checkpoints to make us feel comfortable as contributors to a group project. Do not hesitate to contact me if these kinds of issues surface in your project group.

If you are working with adult or professional students, or students with extensive experience with more group projects in their courses, you could create an assignment for the purpose of eliciting their analysis of the group process. Alternatively, you could ask students to analyze articles or case studies as the basis for a comparative assignment. Here is an example you can adapt for your needs:

Collaboration Effectiveness Analysis

- Organization or Course Name and Brief Description
  - Types of teams or collaborative groups
  - Types of tasks or projects
  - An ineffective example
  - Description of the team or group
  - Your reasons for believing the group was not effective
  - An effective example
  - Description of the team or group
  - Your reasons for believing the group was effective
  - Compare and contrast these work groups or teams. What recommendations do you have to improve effectiveness or address other problems, such as the ways that participants communicate or organize their work?

By asking students to discuss their prior experiences from the beginning, you have a chance to acknowledge and respond to specific concerns. After doing so you can do the following:

- Take into account individual differences in motivation and skills.
- Provide access to relevant information or resources that could help the student better understand the reasons why problems emerge in collaborative work and find ways to address any issues.
- As appropriate, remove constraints or add new levels of control.

Trust and Safety in Collaborative Work

Successful collaboration happens when students trust the instructor, each other, and the fairness and relevance of the assignment. As noted in chapter 3, trust is foundational for collaborative learning. What does this mean for the design of projects and assignments? How can we plan learning experiences that encourage students to trust each other and to trust us as their instructors? When I asked research participants, "Why do you think the collaborative e-learning was a success?" issues of trust and safety commonly emerged as the most important factor for success. Research participants described a safe learning environment as one where there are "no silly questions," a place where students can "have wild ideas, be creative and innovative." One participant pointed out that instructors need to "reduce stakes for participation to the point that people do not perceive a high risk for failure or perceive that not succeeding to the highest degree is a learning opportunity, with no comebacks or humiliating criticism." One research participant used a statement in the syllabus to reinforce from the outset of the course the importance of making mistakes in the class to avoid making them in professional life later on, when they could be very costly.

A safe learning environment allows learners to build relationships and gain the trust needed to share ideas and work together. Research participants believed that the instructor has an important role in creating this kind of atmosphere. They described the use of the constructivist principle of scaffolding, in which learning activities build progressively. They talked about taking "baby steps" that "gently walk learners" into the collaborative activities. They discussed starting with "low-risk activities that encourage a sense of group" by inviting everyone to participate. No grades were given for these foundational activities.

Instructor and Facilitator Roles

Instructors or facilitators can take very different roles when students are engaged collaboratively (see Figure 5.2). The first and most important role is as a model of reliability. Students, particularly those with little prior experience, need to feel confident that the instructor is available to troubleshoot and address any problems that arise. This role is essential whether you are adopting instructor-driven, balance, facilitation, or student-driven styles. In an instructor-driven or guided facilitation approach, the instructor can make sure that attention to trust building is included in the project schedule when students have little prior acquaintance before launching into a collaborative project.

We are accustomed to outlining our expectations for students' performance in the syllabus and other materials. An approach I have used successfully involved outlining, very clearly, the expectations for students in the collaborative project and the expectations they can have of me. For example, student expectations for the collaborative project included the following:

- Create an agreement that spells out roles and timing for completion of project deliverables.
- Determine and observe fair distribution of work and protocols for communication.
- Report on team progress each week.
- Address conflicts or problems; request help if not successful.
- Complete quality work on time.

To demonstrate the mutual responsibility and reciprocity essential to collaboration, I also laid out expectations of the instructor. I assured them that they could count on me to do the following:

- Review work in progress.
- Provide detailed feedback on draft.
- Assist as requested on team process.

As you can see, I tried to spell out the importance of developing a plan at the outset and regularly monitoring the progress and participation of collaborative partners. They were expected to make an effort to address issues that arose within the group, but to avoid allowing those issues to derail the project. I made sure they understood that it was their responsibility to contact me if someone was not participating or other problems arose. I reinforced my

Figure 5.2. Instructional styles continuum: Building trust.

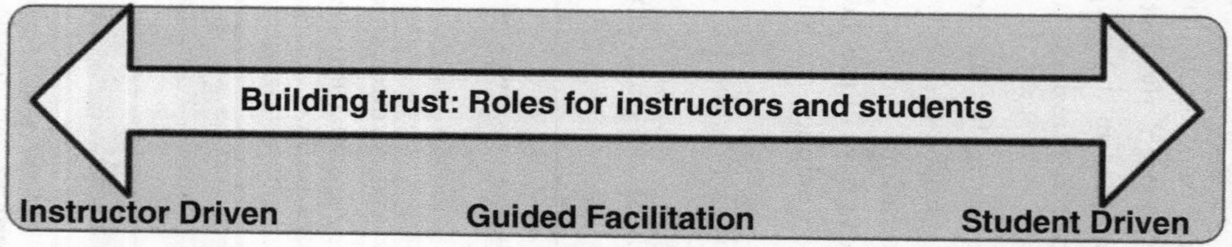

Instructor Driven	Guided Facilitation	Student Driven
Build personal trust between instructor and students by communicating regularly, answering questions, trouble-shooting problems, and offering timely guidance.	**Build personal trust between instructor and students and among students** by facilitating discussions with students, including addressing any fears about the collaborative assignment. Organize dyad or small group exercises to prepare for larger projects.	**Build personal trust among students** by creating a safe classroom environment and providing tools and resources they can choose from, based on their needs.
Build strategic trust with doable assignments, thoughtfully styled groups, clear directions, and relevant resources.	**Build strategic trust** with doable assignments, thoughtfully styled groups, clear directions, and relevant resources.	**Build strategic trust** with challenging assignments that respect students' initiative and allow enough time for trial and error.

role as the person who would provide feedback and support along the way and respond to any requests for help. Here is an excerpt from an announcement posted in the learning management system for an online course:

> This assignment may call into question my role as your instructor. I want to, to the greatest degree possible, turn you loose with this assignment. If you struggle with something, finding your own solution will be a learning experience. At the same time, I am here. You can post in your folder or e-mail me if you have a question or need me to help in some way. If someone is really not responding and not fulfilling their part of the assignment, let me know and we can work together to determine the best action to take.

In many years of teaching this way, few students have contacted me with problems; however, knowing that accountability for others was not fully their responsibility built confidence in the process. Clearly, teaching and supporting collaborative learning is a balancing act. And like many balancing acts, it may tilt one way or another throughout the term. If students become distracted by the process needed to manage the collaborative project, they may fall behind in the acquisition of knowledge and skills associated with the content area of the course. On the other hand, if the project is structured to allow greater focus on the content of the course, students do not have the opportunity to learn the skills needed to plan and manage a collaborative process.

Setting: Online, Face-to-Face, or Blended?

According to social constructivist theory, learning occurs when students interact with each other and with their environment. What are the defining characteristics of the setting for collaborative learning experiences? Are you designing collaborative learning opportunities for online, face-to-face, or learning experiences that will blend face-to-face and technology-mediated interactions?

In today's work world, most of us experience the same kinds of delineations. Some of us work remotely, communicating electronically with others in our organizations across town or across the globe. Some work in face-to-face offices, where we see our coworkers on a regular basis, sit down together for meetings, and perhaps share social activities outside work. Others work in a blended situation to some degree. They may work out of the home office or satellite location part of the time but still visit a main office for some work activities or meetings. Or they may work from a main office, but interact regularly with coworkers, vendors, or others who are located elsewhere. When they work collaboratively, people in these circumstances have to decide which parts of the project can be readily completed from a distance, and when they need richer communication, the ability to show materials or work in progress, and the ability to solicit an immediate response from collaborating partners. They have to decide when it is advantageous to meet face-to-face, whether that means meeting in person or meeting via some synchronous technology. They have to decide the best way to organize their work so they can optimize the time they spend together and the time they're working on the project on their own. Clearly, part of learning how to collaborate entails building a repertoire of strategies that can be used in various settings.

One way to prepare students for real-world decision-making is by considering milieu that extend beyond the classroom. The term *milieu* refers to the setting or environment for the class. Milieu is one of the four commonplaces of education described by Joseph Schwab (1983): learner, instructor, curriculum, and milieu. Novak and Gowin (1984) described interrelationships among the commonplaces: "The milieu is the context in which the learning experience takes place, and it influences how the teacher and student come to share the meaning of the curriculum" (p. 6). The milieu influences not only the place where collaborative learning occurs but also the nature of the learning experience. These ways are distinguished broadly as internal milieu (within the classroom) and external milieu (outside the classroom). In addition, we need to be aware of the broader sociocultural milieu on learner attitudes.

Collaborative projects can be designed to take place at one or more learning milieux (see Figure 5.3) such as the following:

- Internal Class: Collaborative activities take place within the class, primarily involving the instructor and students who interact in the physical classroom or course management system.
- External Organization: Collaborative activities take place outside the classroom, in a business, organization, agency, school, or other site. Such activities could typically involve other people or organizations in the community where the learner lives and works.
- External Web: Activities take place outside the physical or learning management system classroom, in the virtual environment via the Internet.

Internal Milieu: In the Classroom

The internal milieu could be the course's learning management system or other electronic meeting place or a physical classroom. Collaborative projects can occur entirely within the internal milieu, or the classroom could be a place for group formation, preparation, and reflection related to projects conducted externally. Whether or not the collaborative assignment takes students out of the classroom, essential dialogue occurs internally. Internal collaborative projects could include collaborative development of a paper or presentation. Instructor-led presentations about concepts or procedures related to the project typically occur within the classroom.

External Milieux: Local and Global

Collaborative projects in local organizations could include field studies, observations, service-learning, or other volunteerism activities. When project collaboration involves students with others outside the class, they occur in external milieux. To differentiate further: Some external activities take place in businesses, organizations, agencies, schools, or other locations in the local community. Adult students might design collaborative projects to be conducted in their workplaces. These external activities are labeled *organization* in Figure 5.3.

Other external activities involve online connections with people or entities that are not located in the local community. Online activities could include collaborations with students or professionals in other institutions or organizations. They could also include service-learning or volunteer projects to aid people or entities and other parts of the world. These external activities are labeled *Web* in Figure 5.3.

Figure 5.3. Typology of learning milieux.

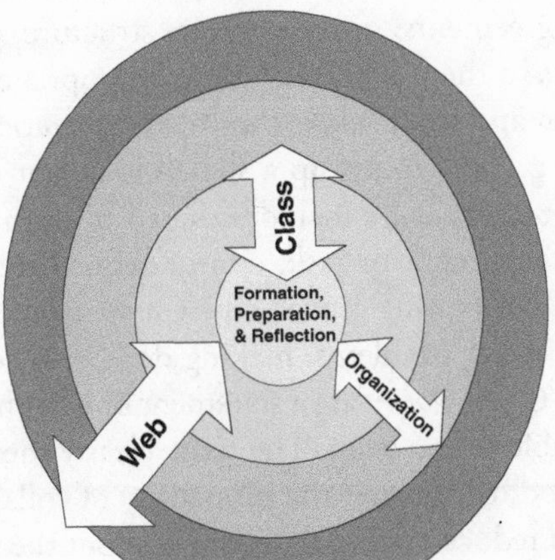

Internal or external collaborative activities can be designed at every stage of the taxonomy of collaboration (see Table 5.1).

Agreements: Laying the Groundwork for Collaborative Learning

Create a climate of trust and belonging. An agreement is the first stage of the collaborative process. The agreement clarifies the expectations of and for the group in terms of goals, roles, key group processes, and climate. One way to ensure that groups create robust agreements is to make it a part of the course requirements. This is particularly relevant when assigning a complex or extended project.

In an instructor-driven situation, or a situation in which time is limited, the instructor might provide a template for students to use. In a balanced facilitation style, the instructor might provide a set of guidelines or required elements that students can use to craft their own agreements. In a student-driven circumstance, the instructor invites the group to write the rules by which they will operate.

The nature of the agreement will depend on the characteristics of the assignment, the length and degree of complexity, and the level of autonomy for student groups to develop their own approaches for completion of the deliverable(s). If every group is completing the same defined project, a simple agreement is adequate. If each group in the class is developing its own project design, with multiple stages and deliverables, a more detailed agreement will be needed. Or if students have little prior experience with managing collaborative projects, a more defined agreement will be helpful. Adapt the recommendations and examples provided in this chapter to fit your circumstances and student characteristics.

Schwab (1983) suggested that four important elements be considered in the discussion of agreements: group context, structure, process, and norms. *Group context* refers to the milieu, including appropriate rewards for performance, information and feedback, technical and material resources, and any training needed (e.g., how to set up a shared folder or use the web conferencing system.) *Group structure* includes shared mission and goals for completing a defined assignment or task, clearly defined roles, clear leadership, or plan for shared or rotating leadership. *Group process* involves protocols and strategies for solving problems, making decisions, communicating, and managing conflict. *Group norms* are a statement of what behaviors are acceptable and unacceptable to the team. The more clearly these norms are articulated and understood, the greater the propensity of collaborative partners to work smoothly and reduce conflict. Decisions about the work design, as laid

TABLE 5.1
Activities in Diverse Milieux

Taxonomy Level	*Class*	*Organization*	*Web*
1. Dialogue	Class or small group discussion is about collaborative processes generally or an assignment/ project in particular.	Students discuss course topics, or the collaborative process, with others in community to gain new insights into ways these ideas translate into practice and the lived experience.	Using web meeting or other tools, students discuss course topics, or the collaborative process, with representatives of groups or external organizations to gain insights from regional, national, or global perspectives.
2. Review	Students review and comment on each other's work in an effort to develop collaborative project or achieve shared goals.	Students receive feedback from others on area of skills development or on some part of a collaborative project.	Students receive feedback from others on area of skills development or on some part of a collaborative project.
3. Parallel	Students divide up group assignment and complete component parts simultaneously.	Students divide up parts of a project that entails working with people or organizations in local settings.	Students divide up parts of a project that entails working with people or organizations using electronic communication.
4. Sequential	Students divide up group assignment and build on component parts in sequence.	Students sequence steps of project to alternate field and classroom activities with collaborative partner or individual research or writing.	Students sequence steps of project to alternate virtual team activities with classroom activities with collaborative partners, individual research, or writing.
5. Synergistic	Students meld their ideas and work together to complete a collective project.	Students research and develop new strategies to address a local or organizational problem or to integrate ideas from diverse perspectives.	Students research and develop new strategies to address a global problem or to integrate ideas from global perspectives.

out in the taxonomy of collaboration, are also part of the group's structures and norms.

If students have the skill levels needed to develop their own format, collaborative partners can answer questions such as the following to craft the style of agreement that works for them:

- What kinds of outcomes are we aiming toward?
- What criteria will we use to assess quality or standards for the outcomes, and what criteria will the instructor use to assess our work?
- What style and form requirements must we observe?
- Who does what, when and how? Do we require all members to contribute equivalent amounts of work?
- Will we capitalize on and enhance the skills of all members?
- What steps or tasks can or should be completed by subgroups or individuals?
- How will subgroup or individual work be integrated with others' work?
- What timing approach will work best for internal communication among collaborative partners?
- Who and what are involved with external communication for projects that extend beyond the classroom, including making sure necessary resources are available?

For online collaboration, additional questions include the following:

- How will we communicate? Synchronous, asynchronous, or both?
- What turnaround time do we expect for response to asynchronous communications?
- In addition to selecting a means for online communication, what tools will we use for iterative writing, resource sharing, and/or archiving of drafts?

The start-up phase of new project groups is critical. It is important to allow the group adequate time, before members are expected to engage in any actual assignment, to decide on the processes that will be used to get the assignment done and the ground rules for how the individuals will behave together. Identifying and planning for the conditions for group effectiveness are important regardless of the instructional style, milieu, or project type.

Agreement Examples

Balanced Facilitation Examples: Learners Determine Format and Steps Within Parameters Set by Instructor

Example 1:
With your group, spell out your answers in a two- to four-page agreement.

1. How will you learn and work together? Will your group primarily use a knowledge acquisition, knowledge transfer, or knowledge cocreation approach?
2. What leadership model will you use (fixed, rotating, shared)?
3. What parts of the project will you complete individually, and what work will you complete together?
4. Will you use parallel, sequential, or synergistic styles in your project? How?
5. How often will your group meet, and in what way will you meet? If your group is meeting virtually, describe what tools or platforms you will use and whether you will meet synchronously or asynchronously.
6. How will you communicate with each other?
7. What are the group's ground rules?

Example 2:
With your group, spell out your answers in a two- to four-page agreement.

1. Clarify the assignment and outline project purpose, objectives, and scope.
   a. Why is the group doing the assignment? What is the purpose of the assignment, and what are the learning objectives and desired project outcomes?
   b. What types of activities will group members be doing, and what are the expected results?
   c. Are you expected to collect data or research information about a problem or opportunity? Are you expected to document the results of an investigation and write a report outlining findings and recommendations?
   d. Are you expected to provide a new idea or design something?
   e. Are you expected to produce some type of document, drawing, model, object, product, prototype, tool, or event?

   f. Are you expected to outline the costs/benefits of your solution or in some way measure results?
2. What are the specific project boundaries and scope?
   a. What are the deadlines and due dates?
   b. What are the project deliverables? (Number of pages, amount of space, number of hours expected to produce, number of outputs, major report sections, etc.)
3. Clarify expectations group members have for themselves and the project.
   a. What skills and knowledge does the group have? Who can provide help and leadership on specific tasks and assignments? Who would like to try something new or different? What resources do group members have that might help the project group?
   b. Who will be fulfilling the formal leadership role? Will the same person lead throughout, or will the role rotate among members? What do the instructor and the group expect of this person? What expectations does this person have of group members?
   c. What would members like to get out of the process? What are each person's specific learning objectives? What benefits could be gained from the project? What concerns and questions do members have?
   d. What will be the consequences if a group member does not complete his/her assignments promptly? What process should the group leader follow to address missing or incomplete assignments? What process will the instructor follow? How can members be reached? Can you distribute or post a roster including phone numbers, e-mail addresses, and other contact information?
4. Decide on the work design and plan.
   a. How will members communicate progress and get together to finalize their deliverables? Will you use shared workspaces, e-mail tracking, telephone calls, threaded conversations, and so on?
   b. How will coordination and reporting duties be handled?
   c. How will additional action items be assigned and completed?
   d. How will discussions and decisions be documented and shared?
   e. How should group members identify and work through conflicts?

Instructor-Driven Examples: Instructor Provides a Template

- Group members:
- Names, roles, and so on.

- Operating logistics and contact information:
- Ground rules:
- Deliverables:
- Membership responsibilities:
- Project work plan:
- Key milestones:
- Detailed tasks:
- Checkpoints:

Group Setup Checklist

Once an agreement has been drafted, a checklist can help students double-check completeness:

- Prepared a preliminary or draft of the project charter, discussed the draft and made necessary revisions, and then submitted the final project charter to the course instructor for approval.
- Distributed or posted a group roster including phone numbers, e-mail addresses, and other contact information (regular mail, fax). Reviewed group member profiles with relevant personal and professional information.
- Developed a group calendar that shows member availability for phone calls, e-mail, and impromptu group meetings.
- Established compatibility of technology and comfort with technology that will need to be used for group interchange and for project work.
- Finalized the modes of communication the group will use (group folder, e-mail, shareware, teleconference, synchronous chat, etc.)
- Completed a group kickoff meeting that included some time for an enjoyable exchange of information and highlights about members' expectations, contributions, and needs. Discussed expected time commitments and completion of assignments and status reports.
- Set group/project ground rules and discussed expected code of conduct for discussion, critique, and feedback. Established guidelines for managing conflicts.
- Discussed grading guidelines and agreed-upon procedures for commenting on individual and group deliverables. Discussed the guidelines for verbal and written feedback.
- Answered the following questions and considerations:
  - Outlined how documents will be created, retrieved, updated, deleted.

- How are drafts created and stored?
- Are authors noted or does the entire group own the documents?
- Who will organize and maintain the documents?
- Who can accept or reject documents?
- How will final documents be distributed?
- If someone speaks a different language, what type of translation assistance may be required?
- What guidelines will be used for writing and formatting documents?
- Agreed upon meetings format for synchronous communication on face-to-face meetings.
- What meeting technologies will be used?
- Who calls the meeting?
- How will agendas be developed and shared?
- Who facilitates the meeting?
- How will documents and information be shared during a meeting?
- How will meeting minutes be handled/distributed?

Summary

All collaborative assignments involve interdependencies among members. However, parallel and sequential teams need to negotiate on logistical bases, whereas synergistic groups must negotiate and collaborate on a more conceptual level. Time, learning objectives of the class or session, availability of groupware or other tools, degree of trust, and characteristics of the learners are some factors to be considered when choosing the most appropriate styles of collaborative teaching and learning. So that everyone understands the requirements and expectations, an initial agreement is essential.

Key Questions: Prompts for Discussion or Reflection

- What kinds of collaborative assignments best fit the curriculum, academic level, and student characteristics in your educational setting?
- What steps will you take to design collaborative learning activities? Will you need to engage with others in your institution to adopt such activities in courses you teach?
- Do your students have access to software or platforms they can use for collaborative projects? Do your students have the digital literacy and technical skills needed to use the collaborative and communications features of these technologies?

- What is the culture of your educational setting? Is the culture accommodating for collaborative work? Are your students accustomed to peer interaction in the classroom? If changes are needed, what will you do to promote them?
- What learning milieu will be the setting for collaborative learning experiences? What opportunities can provide learning experiences outside the classroom?

6

ASSESSING COLLABORATIVE LEARNING

We meet because the knowledge and experience needed in a specific situation are not available in one head, but have to be pieced together out of the knowledge and experience of several people.

—Peter Drucker, 2006

Objectives

Chapter 6 will prepare you to:

- Differentiate between formative and summative assessments.
- Consider ways to use informal and formal feedback with individuals and groups.
- Design and use assessments for individual and/or collective outcomes.
- Develop assessment protocols or rubrics appropriate for assessing collaborative processes.

Introduction

Chapter 5 recommended ways to design assignments and articulate objectives that encompass collaborative learning in both content and process areas. In chapter 6, we will look at options for assessing the degree to which students meet those objectives. Traditionally, instructors thought about student assessment primarily in terms of grading individual students on their own performance. Today assessment is seen as a progressive process that continues throughout the course, rather than an accounting of outcomes at the end. Employing ongoing, multipronged assessment is essential when students are engaged in collaborative work that may entail activities outside the brick-and-mortar classroom, such as online interactions, fieldwork, or service-learning in the local community.

First, some basic definitions for terms used in this chapter. The word *assessment* is used broadly to describe processes used to determine the success of learners in achieving learning goals. While assessment is sometimes used interchangeably with the word *evaluation*, this term typically refers to processes used to determine success of the program, curriculum, or course.

The term *outcomes* refers to the deliverables (e.g., papers or presentations) and the measurable learning (e.g., improved knowledge, skills, or abilities) that result from the collaborative learning experience.

Formative assessment is the type of assessment used to provide instructors and learners with information about how well students are progressing in order to help both improve performance. There are many ways in which instructors can provide feedback to assist the development of student learning. The important issue is that whatever the selected method, it must be able to provide information about what the student does and does not know, as well as specific direction for improvement.

It can include the following:

- monitoring work on a regular basis, making sure to spell out frequency or timing for instructor monitoring as part of the course or project expectations;
- ascertaining needs for additional resources, guidance, or revisions; and
- determining whether all participants are contributing and whether the agreements and time lines are being observed.

Summative assessment is used to gather evidence needed to assign grades. It can include the following:

- comparing results with criteria derived from expectations and objectives;
- identifying common problems that point to the need for clearer objectives, assignment guidelines, or instructional approaches; and
- giving fair grades that take into consideration all aspects of the assignment.

Grading refers to the formal, quantitative measure of success in relation to the goals and standards. We need to offer students timely responses using a fair, explicit, and systematic process when assessing collaborative work.

Feedback can be formal or informal, written or verbal, formative or summative. Feedback can encompass personal messages of encouragement as well as evaluative passages about students' work. Bauer and Williamson (2014) describe two classes of feedback that can help to align formative and summative assessments. One is *task-level feedback* that relies on evidence gleaned about the task(s) on which the students are working. The authors suggest that this kind of feedback can be provided while work on a particular task is underway, upon completion of any intermediate work products, or after the students have completed a task. The second type Bauer and Williamson (2004) highlight is what they call *summary feedback* on the development of students' knowledge, skills, and abilities. This type is distinct from summative assessments in that the individual or group of students may acquire new knowledge, skills, and abilities beyond those directly associated with assignment tasks.

While each of these types has a specific purpose, in some situations educators will use all of them. Educators choose their priorities and decide where to focus their attentions. In some situations, formative feedback takes precedence because students need input and guidance throughout an extended project. In other situations, summative feedback and grading are needed to keep students on track. Such students need the reassurance of satisfactory grades to keep going because uncertainty about how their work will be measured is counterproductive to success with a collaborative project. With planning and mutual accountability, assessment can become an avenue for meaningful communication—resulting in a better experience for instructors and students. The "learning to collaborate, collaborating to learn" system of thinking has implications for student assessment. Importantly, if we want students to learn *how* to collaborate, we need to assess the degree to which they meet expectations for participation in the collaborative process used to complete the assignment.

The ways students will be assessed should be spelled out in the syllabus, the learning objectives, and the assignment instructions. The need for clarity at the outset cannot be overstated. Clear guidelines and information about assessment are important for students who are venturing into collaborative work that may be unfamiliar to them. This is even more important in online classes, where students may not have friendly or social relationships with collaborative partners or opportunities for informal conversations with instructors. Students will feel more confident if they know what to expect and in particular how they will be assessed and graded.

Assessment and Collaborative Learning

Collaborative learning can potentially generate individual and collective outcomes. Or assignments can be designed to include a collaborative experience, with individual outcomes. Instructors who are teaching with collaborative methods are thus responsible for assessing individual and group achievement with content and collaborative process. The accomplishment of a task together is inherent to most collaborative learning assignments. Students actively communicate and work together to produce a single outcome, talking and sharing their cognitive resources to establish joint goals and referents, to make joint decisions, to solve emerging problems, to construct and modify solutions, and to evaluate the outcomes through dialogue and action (Hennessy & Murphy, 1999). The assignment could ask them to produce one project, paper, or presentation that represents everyone's efforts. This can be described as a *collective outcome* of a collaborative process. Students working collaboratively can be asked to reflect on the experience in a journal or an essay or to complete some increment of the project independently. The product of this solo work is referred to here as an *individual outcome* of a collaborative process. Individual and collective assessment are complementary and allow instructors to encourage individual achievement while promoting a culture of shared purpose and learning community.

A fundamental challenge for instructors who use collaborative methods is to find a balance between rewarding individual performance and promoting group interdependence. How can instructors use formative and summative assessments and informal feedback to encourage individual initiative and fair contributions by all members of the group? Three goals for assessment of collaborative work are to make sure that work is fairly distributed among collaborative partners, to give feedback that supports group performance, and to assess both individual and collective processes and outcomes. The way that we achieve these goals may vary depending on time available for the activity, the instructional style, and the curricular goals and nature of the subject matter.

Taxonomies, Models, and Assessment Strategies

Chapter 1 introduced three frameworks: the collaborative knowledge learning model, Bloom's taxonomies for affective and cognitive domains, and the taxonomy of online collaboration. Each framework gives us a different lens through which to assess collaborative learning. To explain the kinds of deliverables and assessments that can be used to understand the progress and achievements of individuals and groups of students, the typology of collaborative learning assessment is introduced. Taken together, these four frameworks give us ways to gain a precise and detailed picture of students' collaborative learning experiences so we can provide needed guidance and measure performance.

Assessment With the Collaborative Knowledge Learning Model or Bloom's Taxonomies

The collaborative knowledge learning model shows ways to align the assignment purpose, characteristics of the students and educational setting, and intended type of knowledge learning. Assessment questions and strategies can be articulated to assess progress in one or more of the four types of collaborative learning: knowledge transfer, exchange, acquisition, and cocreation.

When the goal is knowledge exchange, learning that occurs when we share information or resources with another person, an initial level of assessment could be fairly straightforward. Did the student provide the other(s) with the kinds of materials spelled out in the assignment, or not? A deeper level of assessment could integrate Anderson and colleagues' (2000) detailed knowledge dimension to differentiate specific types of knowledge exchange:

- Did the student(s) provide facts the partners need to move forward with the collaborative assignment?
- Did the student(s) provide concepts, with appropriate categories, classifications, theoretical frameworks, and so on that the partners need to move forward with the collaborative assignment?
- Did the student(s) share procedures, techniques, or methods the partners can use move forward with the collaborative assignment?
- Did the student(s) provide strategic metacognitive knowledge the partners need to advance with the collaborative assignment?

For example, let's consider a collaborative project assignment that asks each group of students to generate three alternative solutions to the problems embedded in a case study, with solutions supported by literature from the field. To assess the group members, the instructor could ask the following questions:

- Did the student(s) read the case carefully to identify key *facts* the partners need to understand the context and parameters of the case?
- Did the student(s) draw relevant *concepts*, with appropriate categories, classifications, theoretical frameworks, and so on, from the case that partners could use as the basis for generating solutions?
- Did the student(s) share procedures, techniques, or methods for analyzing or addressing the problems? Did the student(s) share with others awareness of their strengths and limitations by sharing metacognitive knowledge with partners?

Using this same assignment as an example, we could similarly articulate assessment questions that focus on types of knowledge students transfer (when one student imparts knowledge to another) or acquire (when students learn new knowledge together). Did students help each other learn the facts, concepts, procedures, and metacognitive awareness needed to unpack the problems in the case study?

Since the assignment asks students to generate solutions to a problem, we can draw on knowledge cocreation principles from the collaborative knowledge learning model, and/or the synthesis or create levels from Bloom's original (1956) or the revised (2000) cognitive domain (Table 6.1). In their explanation of the create category, Anderson and colleagues (2000) emphasize that a task of this kind requires aspects of each of the earlier cognitive process categories to some extent. They suggest three phases, each of which can be assessed: problem generation, solution planning, and solution execution. In the given example in which the assignment asks students to generate solutions, students would focus on understanding and framing the problem and then drawing on many sources to recommend novel ways to address it. Students could arrive at their solutions using higher levels of thinking.

TABLE 6.1
Assessment and Bloom's Cognitive Domain

Level	*Questions to Guide Assessment at Each Level*
Remember	Does the student know the terminology and concepts used to explain the collaborative process?
Understand	Can the student create meaning from messages received from the instructor and collaborative partners? Can the student interpret, classify, summarize, and explain the content associated with the assignment and the collaborative process used to complete it?
Apply	Can the student implement the steps and assignment tasks agreed to with collaborative partners?
Analyze	Can the student analyze the research, drafts, descriptions of experiences, and so on contributed by collaborative partners and organize and integrate them as needed to complete the assignment?
Evaluate	Can the student judge research contributions by collaborative partners based on criteria established by the instructor or the group?
Create	Can the student work collaboratively with others to generate or develop new solutions, ideas, or approaches that incorporate contributions by the group and meet requirements for the assignment?

Assessing Learning Activities Associated With Each Level of the Revised Bloom's Taxonomy for the Cognitive Domain

To accomplish higher levels of collaboration, students will need to develop trust in each other's willingness and ability to do the background research needed as the basis for the interpretation and remedy they will put forward together in response to the case. Developing trust is also associated with development of values. To assess these characteristics, we can draw on the affective domain of Bloom's taxonomy (Table 6.2).

TABLE 6.2
Assessment and Bloom's Affective Domain

Level	*Questions to Guide Assessment at Each Level*
Receiving phenomena: Is aware and willing to listen	To what extent does the student listen to the instructor, collaborative partners, and others working on the project? To what extent does the student listen to others with different perspectives on the phenomenon at hand?
Responding to phenomena: Attends and reacts to a particular phenomenon	To what extent does the student respond appropriately to messages received from the instructor and collaborative partners? Is the student sensitive to individual and cultural differences? Does the student value diversity?
Valuing: Attaches worth or value and builds commitment	To what extent does the student value and commit to the collaborative partners, process, and agreements?
Organizing: Compares, relates, synthesizes values; creates priorities among conflicting values	To what extent does the student accept or resolve differences in values among collaborative partners or others associated with the project? To what extent does the student revise judgements based on new evidence? To what extent does the student develop/use systematic planning in solving problems that arise in the collaboration?
Internalizing values: Has a value system that guides behavior	To what extent does the student adopt a value system that includes respect for collaborative partners, agreements, and processes? To what extent does the student exemplify a spirit of collaboration?

Source. Adapted from Bloom, Krathwohl, & Masia, 1964. *Taxonomy of educational objectives: Handbook II: Affective domain.* New York: David McKay.

Assessment With the Typology of Collaborative Learning Assessment

The instructor can assess individual deliverables such as an annotated bibliography of the research each student conducted, and the instructor can assess the collective outcomes generated by the group. A typology of collaborative learning assessment was constructed to categorize assessment approaches (see Table 6.3). These approaches can be combined as appropriate given the nature of the assignment and the potential presence of other external stakeholders in practica, fieldwork, service-learning, or other community-oriented projects. The typology of collaborative learning assessment includes seven options for assessment of individual or collective outcomes.

In some cases, collaborative projects may include both collective outcomes (the paper, presentation, or project created by the group) and individual outcomes (a report, journal, or paper). Some assignments involve a collaborative learning experience, but individual outcomes. For example, a small group could conduct a research project together but each person writes an individual paper. For such assignments, the assessment focuses on both the collective experience of the collaborative process and participation and the individual outcome.

These options can be combined to fit the particular assignment. The first category is self-assessment. Reflection is one of the processes named in the taxonomy of online collaboration, and the value for assessment is one of the reasons for including it. Even in a collaborative assignment completed in a physical classroom where the instructor can see small groups' activities, some steps are inevitably carried out beyond the classroom. Self-assessment can make these activities available for the instructor to review. Furthermore, the metacognitive and cognitive processes students use to make sense of the group experience are not necessarily visible to the instructor. Self-assessment can take an open-ended narrative form, as in journal entries, or it can take a more concise form, as in the checklist. Self-assessment can be conducted by individual collaborative partners or by the group.

The second category is external assessment, which is important for learning activities that extend beyond the classroom into the local community or the online world. Collaborative learning activities that involve conducting research, practicing new skills, or offering services are typically coordinated with an organization, a school, or an agency. A representative from that setting likely observes the work of the student groups and can provide real-world insight into their performance. Once again, this formal or informal assessment can be aimed at individuals or at the group. For a service-learning or fieldwork project, reports from the external stakeholders or supervisors

TABLE 6.3
Typology of Collaborative Learning Assessment

Type	*Description*
1. Self-assessment (individual)	Individual self-assessment takes place when the learner provides his or her own assessment of performance. • Journal entries • Individual progress report or checklist • Verbal discussion in meeting or check-in with instructor
2. Self-assessment (collective)	Collective self-assessment takes place when the team or group assesses their own process and outcomes. • Team progress report or checklist • Update or revision to work plan • Summary of work process • Verbal discussion in meeting or check-in with instructor
3. External assessment (individual)	When the collaborative assignment extends beyond the classroom to include community projects, service, or volunteerism, external supervisors, mentors, or stakeholders can assess an individual student's performance. • Narrative comments on journal entries or reports • Verbal comments • Feedback form, checklist, or questionnaire
4. External assessment (collective)	When the collaborative assignment extends beyond the classroom to include community projects, service, or volunteerism, external supervisors, mentors, or stakeholders can assess the group's performance. • Verbal comments in call or meeting with the instructor • Feedback form, checklist, or questionnaire
5. Instructor assessment (individual)	The instructor assesses individual achievement in the context of the collaborative assignment. • Review comments, suggestions, or recommendations provided verbally or in writing.
6. Instructor assessment (collective)	The instructor assesses collective outcomes according to the level of the group's achievement. • Review comments, suggestions, or recommendations provided verbally or in writing.
7. Grading	The instructor uses numerical or alphabetical scores to communicate a quantitative measure in relation to the assignment's goals and standards.

can complement the team's self-assessment. The third category is instructor assessment of individual efforts and group achievement, in relation to the expectations and requirements of the assignment and in relation to the group's own agreements and work plans. The last category is grading, the number or letter used to indicate the measure given to the final completion of the work.

The typology of collaborative learning assessment can be applied in summative or formative ways. Formative assessment can reinforce positive behaviors and help build students' confidence in their ability to successfully complete collaborative work. One goal of formative assessment for individuals is to show how their work builds on and complements others' ideas. One goal of collective formative assessment is to create a sense of learning community—to help learners see how their individual pieces add up to something greater when they collaborate. Comments reflecting group work back to them can help students see that areas where they have strengths may also be areas where others need to grow. Students gain a sense of purpose for participation when they see specific ways they can learn from and with others. Instructors can use formative feedback sessions to help troubleshoot problems within the group. Formative assessment for individual learners can help them resolve to fit with the group, even when personal relationships, or rapport are less than ideal.

Types of Summative Comments

The community of inquiry model offers a good framework for thinking about the types of comments you want to give, to achieve what purpose (Garrison, 2017). Instructors might want to build social presence to foster trust, connection, and a collegial environment with students on a personal level. Comments that build social presence include motivational statements that affirm successful aspects of individual or group work. Such comments help students to see why it is important to participate in and contribute to the collaborative process, even when it might be difficult to do so. When trying to build social presence, instructors may find they connect with the affective domain by encouraging students to value each other's efforts. Instructors might want to show cognitive presence by encouraging students to construct new meanings. Or instructors might see the need for teaching presence because students need information and guidance. Comments to build cognitive and teaching presence might invite students to elaborate on the ideas presented. Questions could include "What are the causes of. . . ?" or "Try answering the question for the point of view of. . . ." Comments that aim for cognitive and instructional presence help students to connect meanings to the larger purpose of course and professional practice. These kinds of comments can help students avoid wasting time by going in the wrong direction. Diagnosing misconceptions and providing explanations is an essential educational responsibility. In an educational context it is important to manage time and not to allow learners to become frustrated to a point they disengage. As a subject matter expert, direction may be needed to help learners become aware of the nuances of the discipline (Garrison, 2006).

Requiring an interim or periodic report for larger assignments or projects can help instructors make sure everything is on track. Group reports are useful as teachable moments in both summative and formative ways. They offer an introduction to conversations and troubleshooting on team process or group performance. Use the report to do the following:

- compare status with projected checkpoints articulated in work plans or agreements;
- reflect on work process—relationships as well as progress toward achieving outcomes;
- identify any performance issues or interpersonal conflicts and request the instructor's guidance;
- recommend updates to the work plan as needed;
- suggest revisions and new checkpoints; and
- offer written or verbal feedback—if possible, schedule a short meeting with each group or their representative.

In the case of a performance issue, the progress report offers an objective way for students and instructors to bring the problem to light so it can be remedied before it can undermine success. Progress reports can be graded, allowing instructors the opportunity to evaluate process as well as outcomes.

Collective Self-Assessment

Group members can benefit from collective self-assessment throughout shorter assignments and at strategic points for larger projects. Collective self-assessment is an excellent way to learn how to collaborate—indeed, instructors should emphasize the value of recognizing successful efforts and developing skills necessary to identify and resolve difficult issues that could obstruct or derail the project.

At the midpoint of the group life cycle, many groups experience transitions in their roles and behaviors. Effective group members pay attention to transitions and candidly assess the health of the group. This kind of self-assessment provides an opportunity to reorganize and rethink how best to achieve the goals of the assignment. Depending on the circumstances of the group, this might be a good opportunity for a check-in or coaching session with the instructor.

Group members may experience conflict over progress (or lack of it), goals, roles, or power struggles. The composition of the group, individual differences in styles, personality, culture, and/or work styles can all be sources of conflict between group members. To recognize the symptoms of ineffectiveness, group members should reflect on the following questions:

- Do some group members dominate most of the conversation?
- Do some group members appear to give in to the group or high-status group members, rather than defending their positions?
- Do some group members appear to be doing most of the work?
- Do some group members appear not to be using information given to them?
- Is the group late with deliverables or missing milestones?

Answers to these questions can help to identify whether conflicts exist and, if so, what type. Conflict within a group can occur in the form of a task, relationship, or process conflict. In *task conflict*, members argue about ideas, strategies, and direction. This type of conflict is not necessarily bad, as it can often lead to the group creating unique outcomes and novel ideas and improving decision-making outcomes. In *relationship conflict*, there is a disagreement based on personal issues or personality clashes, which can interfere with group effectiveness. This type of conflict might reduce the effort put toward the group. In *process conflict*, group members disagree about how to perform the task or who should take which role.

Individual Self-Assessment

Individual self-assessment is important throughout the entire collaborative process. These reflective activities enable students to monitor their own responses to the group and think through developmental needs. Individual self-assessment can take place through a reflective journal. A checklist such as the one in Table 6.4 offers a quick way to consider strengths and identify developmental needs.

TABLE 6.4
Self-Assessment Example

Support Group Work			
1. Participate in developing a work agreement			
2. Work to remove barriers to collaboration			
3. Value the contributions of all group members			
4. Acknowledge and celebrate group accomplishments			
5. Share credit with others			
6. Foster effective give-and-take relationships			
Build Your Group			
7. Honor the work agreement, communicate with others if problems arise that might cause a delay			
8. Contribute to a shared vision and shared goals			
9. Help facilitate effective interactions among group members			
10. Build positive shared values and group norms			
11. Participate in collective self-assessment			
12. Honestly assess your own participation in the group			
Develop Group Collaboration Skills			
13. Decide when to use a group approach for problem-solving			
14. Help improve the group decision-making process			
15. Seek involvement of the instructor or field project supervisor as needed			

TABLE 6.4 *(Continued)*

Three behaviors I will work on developing: 1. 2. 3.

Self-Assessment and Reflection

Reflect on your roles and experiences with collaborative activities outside of this class and within your project group. Ask yourself whether each of these behaviors is currently a strength for you or needs development. Record relevant notes or examples. Choose the three behaviors that you feel you most need to develop.

Strategies for Assessment With the Taxonomy of Collaboration

The following examples offer ways to fairly assess students' collaborative work.

Example 1: Learning Activity With Collaborative Teamwork and Collective Outcomes

This blended service-learning project involves a series of steps throughout the semester that center on collective work in small groups (Figure 6.1). Each team works with a local nonprofit organization to create a set of communication plans and resources; they create one collective outcome that represents the work of the entire group. Individuals complete elements of the project and reflect on the group process throughout the semester.

Project steps (Figure 6.1) are summarized as follows:

1. Students are assigned to groups and given an agreement template to fill out.
2. Group members work in parallel to research nonprofit agencies as potential partners with whom to conduct the project.
3. Group members have a dialogue about group process and completion of the agreement. They dialogue about the research each of them completed as the basis for the project.
4. Group members work synergistically to determine their criteria and select a nonprofit agency setting and develop interview questions to ask the agency staff in order to assess the needs. They develop an internal proposal memo to communicate decisions and plans to the agency and the instructor.

5. Groups post their internal proposals on the class blog and then comment on at least one other group's proposal. Students choose the best proposal using the rubric to assess whether they meet requirements for a clear statement of purpose, analysis of agency's probable writing needs, organization, format, and style.
6. Groups work synergistically to use what they learn from peer feedback to improve or revise proposals before submitting them to the instructor for review.
7. Project deliverables are crafted synergistically and presented to the agency supervisor and the instructor. A final report is completed about the project. Individuals reflect on their own work as members of the group and in relation to the service project.

Learners do both individual and team writing throughout this project. Individual writing includes a decision-maker memo to the instructor and an e-journal in which the writer reflects on learning from the course content and the collaborative process. Together group members create an executive summary, a press release, or another deliverable the agency has requested. They also work together to create progress and final reports.

Assessment has an additional dimension for service-learning, internships, or other educational activities that take place outside the classroom. Depending on the nature of the project, formative and summative assessments by representatives of the site are essential. Their input is particularly important when students are developing a project intended to meet a need identified by the organization, school, agency, or other site. Expectations for

Figure 6.1. Learning activity with collaborative work and collective outcomes.

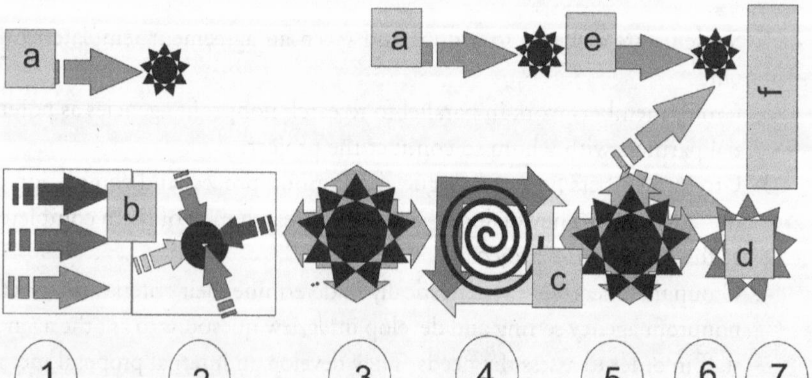

the site project supervisor should be clearly spelled out from the design stage of the project. Are site supervisors expected to provide some level of assessment for individuals engaged in the project, the group, or both? Are they expected to provide formative assessments while the project is underway or to simply provide summative assessment on the project at its completion? In this example, the external representative is actively involved in the assessment process.

Assessments in all categories are integrated throughout the sequence of course activities.

- Formative and Summative, Individual: Two writing conferences, one-on-one with student and instructor, are scheduled throughout the term. These meetings allow for discussion of the student's self-assessment in conjunction with the instructor's assessment and feedback.
- Formative and Summative, Collective: Using a template provided by the instructor, each group submits a weekly progress report to ensure that any problems can be addressed immediately. The report includes discussion of success, frustrations, and steps completed on task assignments. The progress report is submitted to the instructor. The section describing progress on project deliverables is also submitted to the site supervisor.
- Formative and Summative, Individual and Collective: The instructor provides constructive feedback about the review process and about the revisions or changes needed based on reviews received from their peers. Participation by individuals is noted as evidence for summative assessment.
- Collective Self-Assessment: Each group pulls together the weekly reports, the project deliverables, and any final comments on the learning and experiences associated with the project.
- Individual Self-Assessment: Each individual provides a final assessment about his or her own and the team's work.
- Grading: Using all of evidence collected throughout the project, the instructor assigns grades to each individual. The instructor decides, based on weekly reports, whether everyone in a particular group will receive the same grade or not.

Example 2: Writing Circle With Collaborative Process and Individual Outcomes

The writing circle exemplar (Figure 6.2) is a multistep collaborative project that results in individual outcomes. The goal of the project is development of

Figure 6.2. Map of a writing circle project.

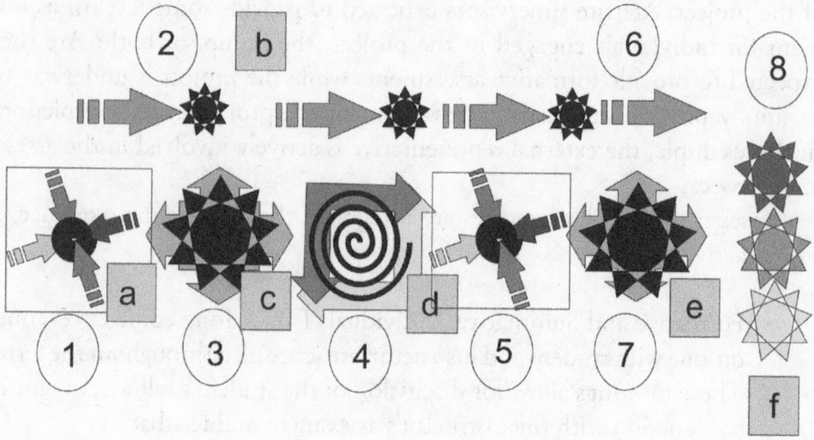

a significant deliverable by each student, such as a research proposal, thesis or dissertation chapter, draft article for publication, or another high-stakes piece of writing. Given the nature of the assignment, it lends itself to graduate-level courses or writing center programs in which students are interested in creating some kind of written deliverable for an external audience. For simplicity, the term *article* is used here to describe the writing deliverable each student is working to develop. In a project like this, collaboration occurs with the process. Students provide encouragement and critical reviews of each other's work, but generate their own individual article drafts. The example describes a hybrid or blended class, but this type of assignment can work in a face-to-face, hybrid, or all e-learning course.

The instructor has two important roles in this kind of project. She is responsible for ensuring the integrity of the process and for using timely, thoughtful, formative feedback assessment to do so. Summative assessment and grading are optional, depending on whether the project is offered as part of a formal academic course or an informal writing class or other professional development session.

Because the collaborative aspect of the writing circle is centered on critiques of each other's work, a high degree of trust and clear review criteria are essential to success. The initial discussion (circle 1) is thus a critical one. It should be conducted synchronously with all in attendance, either face-to-face or in an online web conferencing space. In this discussion, students get acquainted and talk about what they hope to achieve with the article they will work on for the project. The instructor discusses the collaborative process and asks students to reflect on what they need from and fear about having their work reviewed by others. Students come to a preliminary agreement about ground rules and what they can expect from each other. At this point (square a), formative and summative assessments are directed at making sure students understand the project and expectations.

Next, students go to their individual writing (circle 2). They take time to reflect on their review needs and prepare recommendations for the review process. Formative assessment at this point (square b) allows the instructor to become familiar with the student's planned article and to offer initial comments on the prospective article.

The group comes together (circle 3) to develop the review criteria they will use as the basis for their peer critiques. They could decide to exclude certain aspects, such as grammar. They could decide whether they want to make a checklist or ask for narrative comments. The review is the heart of the project, so synergistic collaboration allows for all to contribute. The instructor facilitates, as needed, and helps to address any sensitive matters. By offering formative assessment (square c), the instructor ensures that the review criteria are clearly articulated and understood by members of the group. The instructor also makes sure that the logistics for review are in place. Will the members send drafts to each other privately as e-mail attachments? Will they post drafts in the forum of a learning management system or a shared drive, where others in the group can view them? The technologies chosen should be accessible to all members and appropriate given any concerns raised by group members.

In parallel to this group process, students work on creating the draft they will submit for peer review. In the peer review stage (circle 4), group members carry out the critiques using criteria and protocols they developed. The instructor is available for questions that may arise during the review exchange. Once completed, the instructor provides formative assessment comments on the draft (square d) and summative assessment on members' efforts to provide timely reviews using criteria and parameters set by the group.

In a group discussion (circle 5), members talk about the experience of giving and receiving reviews, and identify lessons learned. This discussion can be conducted synchronously, either in person or in an online web conferencing space, or asynchronously in a learning management system forum. In follow-up to the review, individuals work to improve drafts in light of the peers' and instructor's comments.

The group comes together for one last time, to synergistically conduct a collective self-assessment of the writing circle (circle 6 and square e). They candidly discuss what worked, what they wish they had known, and what they would do differently in a future writing circle. They can use the assignment map to highlight decision or problem points.

The final draft is prepared (circle 7) for submission (circle 8). The final assessment can be formative, with comments about next steps, and summative, to measure progress in completion of requirements. Depending on the class setting, the instructor can incorporate assessments carried out during the project into the final grade or certificate of completion.

In summary, the writing circle assignment steps are as follows:

1. Groups are formed and begin discussion of the project assignment. They start with a dialogue about writing circle goals. They agree on group process and expectations of members. All members are present and participate in discussion. All members sign on to the charter.
2. Each individual student begins drafting the article. Individuals may also be asked to create a journal and to use it to reflect on review needs and fears.
3. The group engages in synergistic decision-making to determine review goals and criteria.
4. Group members offer critical reviews of each other's drafts.
5. Discussion of review: What are common themes or issues? Are there questions for the instructor?
6. Individuals complete and proofread the final draft, integrating review comments and tips from the discussion. Individuals reflect on group process and the writing circle experience.
7. The group meets to discuss their work and what they learned from the collaborative process.
8. Individuals submit the article for the instructor's formative, summative assessments and grading as appropriate for the course setting.

Next, the summary of writing circle assessment steps is as follows:

- Formative and Summative, Individual: Members are present and participate in discussion.
- Formative and Summative, Collective: All members sign on to the charter.
- Formative, Individual: Article content, reference list, length, and format fit assignment requirements.
- Formative, Individual: Feedback on the review of peer's article. Feedback on suggestions made in review, guidance on ways to use the suggestions to improve the article.

- Formative: Feedback on revised draft.
- Summative, Individual: Members provide timely reviews using criteria and parameters set by the group.
- Formative, Collective Self-Assessment: Members review what they have completed and how, and they troubleshoot overall project.
- Formative: Feedback on final article. Grading Individual: Grade final article as well as the quality of peer reviews, participation in the group.

Example 3: Blended Learning Seminar: Collaborative Process and Collective Outcomes

Next is a blended or hybrid learning example in the form of a seminar. Students in this seminar work in small groups to complete a project collaboratively. To maximize the potential for blended learning, the preparation and postmeeting activities take place online in conjunction with a face-to-face learning event. Online activities utilize asynchronous communication via e-mail, a threaded discussion on a learning management system or private social media group, or synchronous meetings using video chat or a web conferencing system. As illustrated in Figure 6.3, steps for the project fit within a coherent sequential framework. In discrete sequential steps, students work together and, at the same time, individually reflect on their learning and make note of relevant points.

Figure 6.3. Map of a blended learning seminar.

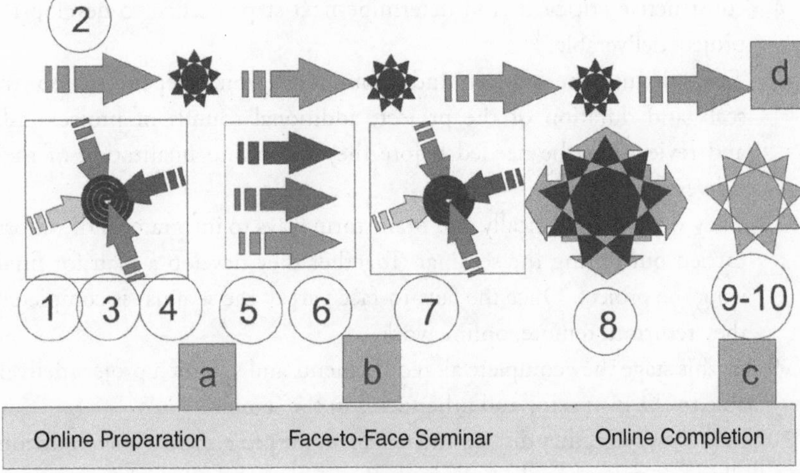

Rich learning experiences are possible when individual and group activities are meshed in an overarching project. Students have the opportunity to achieve curricular objectives while developing skills that will be beneficial in professional life. They can learn how to structure and complete a significant project with collaborative partners, and they can learn how to do so whether they work together face-to-face or remotely.

A summary of seminar steps, as shown in Figure 6.3, follows:

1. Online seminar preparations begin with a dialogue to introduce participants to the content and to each other. The instructor uses an introductory discussion to establish a culture of trust and respect, as well as to clarify expectations for participation in all stages of the seminar.
2. Participants do their own individual preparations, including reading course materials and beginning a reflective journal.
3. Groups are formed and begin discussion of the project assignment.
4. Face-to-face seminar activities (steps 4–8) build on participants' preseminar preparation. Since they arrive with preliminary introductions to each other and a basic understanding of seminar content, goals, and expectations, they are ready to engage with substantive inquiry and to initiate the project in their small groups.
5. They divide up project tasks and determine criteria for the various elements of the project. Depending on the size of the project group, they could complete initial project tasks as individuals or dyads.
6. The tasks completed in parallel are reviewed by others in the project group for critique and commentary. They give each other feedback and constructive criticism, and determine next steps needed to develop the project deliverable.
7. They discuss the project and group evolution. Depending on the scale and duration of the project, additional rounds of project tasks and review may be needed before they move into finalization of their deliverable.
8. They work synergistically and brainstorm ways to integrate all the efforts carried out during the seminar. Together they develop a plan for finalizing the project. Once the face-to-face part of the seminar is completed, they return to remote, online work.
9. At this stage they complete all requirements and submit a project deliverable to the instructor and other peers in the seminar.
10. In the last stage, they discuss and reflect on the project as a whole. Individually, each student finalizes the journal with thoughts about the experience.

Together, they discuss the project as a small group, or with others who participated in the seminar. After the seminar, the instructor might encourage participants to further integrate and apply seminar content as they transition back into their individual studies. Through end-of-project dialogue the instructor can reinforce key learnings, offer follow-up resources, and provide closure.

This kind of seminar model offers many assessment opportunities of all types and could be adapted for an academic (graded) course, a field or service-learning project, or a professional/practical learning environment (ungraded).

A summary of seminar assessment steps in a graded course follows; refer to Figure 6.3.

a. Formative and summative assessments will help individuals shift from the online preparation to the face-to-face seminar events. Formative comments can reinforce the value of discussion contributions and help stimulate insights on the initial ideas shared in individual journals. If students express reluctance or concerns about the collaborative project, they can be addressed at an early stage. At this point, summative assessment may simply involve making note of completion of required activities.
b. The midpoint of the face-to-face seminar would be a good time for another phase of assessment. At this stage the instructor can look at individual journals and offer formative comments and summative notes. The instructor can look at early project work, meeting minutes, group records, and other signs of progress demonstrated in stage 5. Instructors can review the critiques offered to collaborative partners in stage 6. Individual and collective self-assessment are also important. How do individuals feel the project is going, in terms of its substance and in terms of group process?
c. The instructor reviews the deliverable(s) submitted by the project partners.
d. The instructor reviews the journal completed by each individual.

In the final discussions and last journal entries, students engage in individual and collective self-assessment.

Assessment in an Ungraded Professional Development Setting

Assessment in the three examples discussed in this chapter focused on combinations of summative and formative approaches instructors can use to form the basis of a system for awarding grades. In a setting where grades are not awarded, such as professional development or adult community education, the need for assessment is different and calls for other ways of thinking.

Challenges particular to informal educational settings include participant retention and follow-through. To some extent, the loss of a member can occur in any setting because people get sick and students drop out for their own reasons. However, the risk is higher in a less structured, ungraded course. When learning activities are carried out by individuals, the group may suffer when some members leave or have gaps in their participation. When learning activities are carried out collaboratively, the loss of a member can mean that someone has made an incomplete contribution and the quality of the final deliverable could suffer. In these situations, the group's charter and agreement and formative assessment from the instructor (or facilitator) are essential to minimize disruption due to group member absences or departures.

Timely feedback can help group members feel a sense of responsibility to the group and to successfully complete the project. Communication channels that invite all members to check in regularly with the project group and the instructor can build community and social presence. In such an environment, members feel valued and make an effort to stick with the project through completion. When loss of a member is unavoidable, the instructor should meet with the group to evaluate the status of the project. It might be necessary to review the team charter and agreement and change task assignments so that no one member is compelled to pick up an excessive addition of work to compensate for the missing member. Depending on the nature of the project, the instructor can work with the group to alter the scope and scale so it is more manageable to complete with fewer members.

Using Rubrics for Formative and Summative Assessments

While we might aspire to provide detailed, personalized formative and summative feedback to each individual student and collaborative group, the time that would require makes it unrealistic. We need to find time-efficient ways to communicate meaningfully, and scoring rubrics can help us do so. *Rubrics* are defined as scoring scales used to assess student performance using task-specific set of criteria (Loewenstein & Mueller, 2016). In addition to time efficiency, the rationale for using grading rubrics includes the following:

- Rubrics convey expectations for the assignment and classify priorities.
- Rubrics communicate clear expectations to learners for group/individual assignments and participation targets.

- Rubrics offer frameworks for consistent grading across the class.
- Rubrics provide a framework for numerical scoring and narrative comments.

In some instructional situations rubrics associated with assignments are developed by course designers and subject matter experts. These kinds of rubrics are often automated and posted within a learning management system. The recommendations offered here are intended for designers or for instructors who are responsible for creating rubrics. These examples might also be helpful for those who create rubrics to use for formative feedback, even though the summative, grading rubrics have been provided or are embedded in the learning management system. Adapt the criteria and point system to meet your assessment needs.

The first stage of the collaborative process is group formation. This stage should involve the development of two types of agreements: a charter that spells out how collaborative partners will relate to and be accountable to one another and a work plan that spells out who will do what, when, how. You might choose to provide templates for your students so they focus their efforts on determining their roles and relationships in light of the assignment. If so, the rubric would reflect these priorities. Group formation rubrics A and B show two approaches. The first rubric, Rubric A (Table 6.5), allows for scores that can be used for grading purposes but focuses more on comments on the group's formation documents and plans.

Beyond the initial formation (Rubric A), instructors can adapt Rubric B (Table 6.6) for a more summative assessment of individual and collective participation by the whole group in a collaborative assignment. Additional criteria can be added to assess specific achievements related to the assignment. The rubric could be complemented with narrative comments for summative assessment on the content or curricular aspects of the deliverables. The questions noted in Table 6.5 can be adapted to a rubric format or used as the basis for articulating summative comments.

Another type of rubric is more oriented toward formative assessment and essentially works as a format for offering comments (Figure 6.4).

The sample narrative rubric in Figure 6.4 breaks down the sections of the assignment and weights them in terms of the importance to the project grade. However, unlike the other rubrics, criteria are not spelled out. Instead, the instructor uses the form to communicate feedback in each area. A form of this kind could be used with individuals or with the entire group of collaborative partners.

TABLE 6.5

Group Formation Rubric A

Criteria (12 total points)	*Sample Comments*	*Score*
Completed a project charter with clear role definitions and ground rules. (3 points)	Roles are clearly defined. Expectations are stated. Ground rules are clear and specific.	3
Completed a project charter that spells out communication and decision-making protocols. (3 points)	You state that your group prefers synchronous communications on a regular basis to check in. You set weekly conference calls—if everyone can't participate in the conference call, will you post minutes of the call in the discussion forum so others can weigh in? How will you deal with a situation where someone frequently misses the call?	3
Provides specific work plan, milestones, and tasks for all members. Specifies how collaboration levels will be used (parallel, sequential, or synergistic.) (3 points)	Work plans are presented. Guidelines for work and submissions are spelled out.	3
Provides a work plan that indicates developmental goals and steps to achieve them. (3 points)	I see that you have not specifically identified skill development goals. Did your group discuss how the roles you are taking will allow you to build new skills in leadership, decision-making, or online communication? Can you update your plan to include developmental goals?	1

TABLE 6.6

Group Formation Rubric B

Evaluation Criteria	*Excellent*	*Proficient*	*Satisfactory*	*Unsatisfactory*
Connection and Formation 10%	Connected with group and demonstrated leadership enabling group to achieve agreements for roles, work plan, process and collaborative completion of assignment. 10	Connected with group and participated in agreement for completing assignment. 9	Connected with group and agreed to work plan. 8	Did not connect with group. 0
Group Process 10%	Participated fully in collaborative process and fulfilled group agreements. Contributed substantively and demonstrated critical thinking skills. Final post made as assigned. 10	Participated fully in group and fulfilled group agreements. Final post made as assigned. 9	Participated in group. Final post made as assigned. 8	Did not participate with group. 0
Project Outcomes 75%	Project fulfills all criteria and demonstrates higher order thinking. 75	Final project is submitted with all criteria met. 70	Final project is submitted with most criteria met. 50	Did not complete project. 0
Project Time Line Observed 5%	Completed on schedule. 5	Completed on schedule. 5	Completed after scheduled due date. 2	No messages posted. 0

Figure 6.4. Assessment template.

Course Goals:

Goal I:

Goal II:

Goal III:

Assignment Expectations

Review Date (or stage, interim or final):

Student/Group:

Final Paper Maximum _____% = _____ Points
_____ Maximum ____ points Criterion 1: • • Comments:
_____ Maximum ____ points Criterion 2: • • Comments:
_____ Maximum ____ points Criterion 3: • • Comments:
_____ Maximum ___ points Criterion 4: • • Comments:

Comments

Score: _____ points (maximum _____ points)

Summary

The issues raised in chapter 6 are not unique to education. In the workplace we are increasingly expected to participate in teams and work groups to collaborate with others who may be physically present or geographically dispersed. We worry about whether our individual contributions will be acknowledged and suitably rewarded. We worry about whether the project will be organized fairly or whether we will end up with more of the work . . . but no more rewards. We worry about the possibility of freeloaders who stand by and let others do the work but bask in the shared satisfaction of team recognition when the project succeeds. We worry about team members who contribute what we consider inadequate or substandard work that lowers the quality of the outcome—an outcome that has our names attached to it. Students enter a collaborative project with these same worries. The taxonomy of collaboration allows instructors to build individual and collective assessment into every stage of the process. See Table 6.7 for suggestions. By planning and facilitating the collaborative work with fair, systematic, and timely assessments, we can greatly reduce participants' fears. In the process, we can teach important skills in teamwork and group process that will benefit students in future academic as well as professional collaborations.

Key Questions: Prompts for Discussion or Reflection

- Think about a collaborative and team project you experienced in academic or professional life. How was success measured? Who assessed your efforts? Do you feel that the assessment took into consideration all relevant factors? If you were assessing a similar project, what criteria would you use?
- If a student revealed difficulties with the collaborative process in journal entries, what steps would you take? Describe approaches you would use in an online or in a face-to-face situation.
- What grading strategies are fair when assessing collective outcomes?
- How do assessment styles described in this chapter compare and contrast with those you typically use?

TABLE 6.7

Assessing Learning Activities Associated With Each Stage of the Taxonomy of Collaboration

	Activities	*Individual*	*Collective*
Dialogue	Students exchange and develop ideas, plans, and strategies with collaborative partners.	Does the student participate in a timely, reciprocal, and respectful fashion? Does the student make appropriate use of technology tools for synchronous or asynchronous discussion?	Does the group achieve their goals, for example decision-making, task allocation, or workable plan for the collaborative project? Does the group take notes or minutes of their meetings, or otherwise keep track of what was said and decided?
Review	Students review and comment on each other's work to see how individual efforts fit criteria for the assignment. In projects with collective outcomes, students use the review process to determine how individual inputs will fit with the project as a whole.	Does each student offer timely, respectful, and constructive comments to peers, based on criteria the instructor or students have agreed to use? Does the student use technology tools (i.e., shared folders) to complete the assignment? Does the student protect the privacy of the peer whose work the student is reviewing?	Does the group devise and conduct a timely review process within the parameters set by the instructor or the assignment? Does the group summarize what was learned by the review in a way that will allow them to use these insights to improve the collaborative project and outcomes?

Parallel	Students divide up group assignment and complete component parts. Depending on the size of the group, tasks may be completed by smaller teams or dyads.	Does the student fulfill the expectations set in the group's agreement about how and when the task should be completed? Does the student fulfill communication responsibilities laid out in the agreement? Does the student alert the group or instructor if a problem arises?	Does the group agree to organize the project in tasks that can be completed separately? Does the group allocate tasks fairly? Does the group set clear expectations for timing and quality of each project component or task?
Sequential	Students divide up group assignment and build on component parts in sequence.	In addition to questions spelled out for parallel collaboration, does the student lay the groundwork for the next stage of the project? Does the student complete the task or segment of the project on time and hand it off as planned?	Does the group agree to organize the project in tasks that can be completed sequentially? Does the group allocate tasks and logical phases? Does the group set clear expectations for realistic timing and standards for completion of each task?
Synergistic	Students work together to complete a collective project. All are involved and provide input to the project.	Does the student participate in all meetings or activities? Does the student complete readings or other prework and come prepared to contribute thoughtfully and creatively? Does the student respect the collaborative process and others in the group?	Does the group agree to work together in a way that involves active engagement in an unfolding process? Does the group allocate adequate time for the process and agree on any synchronous meetings? Does the group set clear expectations for each collaborative partners' contribution?

7

USING THE TAXONOMY TO MAP ASSIGNMENTS AND ASSESSMENTS

Objectives

After studying chapter 7, you will be able to do the following:

- Define and explain *visual communication.*
- Use the taxonomy of collaboration vocabulary to communicate visually.
- Align checkpoints and assessments with visual assignment maps.

Introduction

Teaching with the taxonomy of collaboration starts with determining how to communicate expectations and key steps with students. A premise of the "learning to collaborate, collaborating to learn" system of thinking is that specific knowledge, skills, and abilities associated with planning, organizing, and managing collaborations can be learned. To fulfill this potential, students can also learn how to communicate about the collaborative process with student partners as well as in future academic and professional collaborations. Communication between instructor and student in academic settings occurs primarily through words—written or spoken. Sometimes, because of the nature of the topic or the complexity of the work at hand, words alone may not be adequate. Visual communication methods, whether used online or face-to-face, can enrich the otherwise word-intensive process of instruction. The visual vocabulary of the taxonomy of collaboration makes it possible to generate assignment or project maps. These maps can be readily shared and used as the basis for explanations about the assignment, alignment with assessments, or troubleshooting problems. By using these approaches, the image becomes a common frame of reference for all parties—instructors, students, external partners, or other stakeholders. This chapter discusses the use of visual communication to augment verbal and textual exchanges when you are using collaborative methods.

Communicate Visually to Engage Students

Advances in technology have made it possible to communicate in more ways. Phones and mobile devices with cameras make it easy to take pictures or video and use drawn or captured images, icons, and emoticons. We can immediately share these visual representations of our realities, so we have become accustomed to visual communications in our everyday lives. We can use these same strategies to communicate with students and in the process teach them to communicate with collaborative partners. Visual maps help to explain steps and affirm shared goals.

Howard Gardner's (1983) theory of multiple intelligences was developed long before we became accustomed to carrying high-powered computers in our pockets. He observed that intelligence comes in many flavors including linguistic, interpersonal, and spatial. While people with linguistic intelligence think in words and people with interpersonal intelligence gain understanding by discussing concepts with others, people with spatial intelligence see and understand meaning through interaction with images and patterns.

Central to spatial intelligence are the capacities to perceive the visual world accurately; to perform transformations and modifications on one's initial perceptions; and to be able to recreate aspects of one's visual experience, even in the absence of relevant physical stimuli (Gardner, 1983).

By using visual maps to communicate strategies for working collaboratively on an assignment and asking students to similarly map their work, students do as Gardner suggests. They transform the visual maps into effective collaborative processes and then transform their collaborative work into visual representations.

The Taxonomy of Collaboration as a Visual Vocabulary

The taxonomy of collaboration has been discussed and demonstrated throughout this book. Now it is your turn to use this framework for your own instructional purposes. First, let's look again at the icons that you will use as a visual vocabulary to create graphics statements.

In the taxonomy of collaboration, the arrows signify the process and the stars signify the outcomes (Table 7.1).

TABLE 7.1
Taxonomy of Collaboration Visual Vocabulary

Icon	*Uses and Meanings*
Reflection 	This icon represents efforts completed individually in the context of the collaborative assignment. Individual work could include reflective journals or other written or creative expressions. This icon can be used to represent any activity individuals carry out in order to make sense of or process events and activities of the collaborative group. Some individual efforts may contribute directly to group work, but in cases where a larger assignment has been broken into pieces that each group member completes, the parallel icon is a more accurate representation.
Dialogue 	This icon represents any activity associated with dialogue. These activities could include discussions with collaborative group members, as well as other stakeholders or supervisors. Dialogues can occur synchronously or asynchronously. If it is important to distinguish between those modes (e.g., when students in hybrid class are planning how they will best use face-to-face time), you could add a note to that effect.
Review 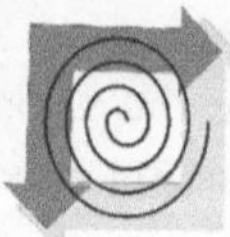	This icon represents the review process. It should be used to signify points in the collaboration when participants critique each other's work or contributions. This icon should be used to represent the stage at which collaborative partners look at elements or components to determine which they will use and how they will fit together. The review could be carried out as a group, in conjunction with a dialogue, or as an exchange of drafts between two collaborative partners.
Parallel 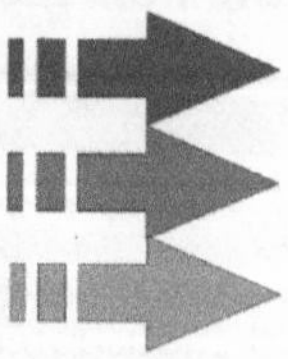	This icon represents segmentation of a project into component parts that can be completed by individuals in the group, or a smaller subgroup, within the same time frame. The kind of work represented by this icon fits within the larger collaborative process that typically involves dialogue, to discuss and plan how and when the work will be completed, and review processes, to examine work products to see whether revisions need to be made. Group members will need to decide how individual components will fit together into collective outcomes or how review comments can be incorporated when the project will result in individual outcomes.

Table 7.1 (*Continued*)

Icon	*Uses and Meanings*
Sequential 	This icon represents segmentation of a project into component parts that can be completed by individuals in the group, or a smaller subgroup, in incremental stages. This icon indicates that stages of the work depend on and build on each other. As described for the parallel icon, sequential designs depend on ongoing dialogue and review. Group members need to decide timing and quality expected for each stage. They also must decide how group members who completed earlier stages will remain involved throughout the entire process, including efforts to mesh components into collective outcomes.
Synergistic 	This icon is used to represent a collaborative process in which all are involved in the work and the assignment is viewed as a whole. This icon is used to represent the types of collaborative process that involve synthesis of individuals' contributions into a collective outcome.
Individual Outcomes 	This icon is used to represent individual outcomes. While collaborative partners typically work to achieve a shared goal and to produce a collective deliverable, it is also possible for group members to collaborate on ideas or approaches, then use what they learn from each other to produce their own deliverables.
Collective Outcome 	This icon is used to represent collective outcomes. This single outcome encompasses the contributions of all participating members of the group.
Feedback or Formative Assessment 	The building blocks icon is used to represent feedback or formative assessment from the instructor or from other stakeholders such as external supervisors for field or service project. You can simply label the places in the process where assessments occur, as is illustrated in chapter 6, or you can use these icons to indicate where formative or summative assessments occur.

(*Continues*)

Table 7.1 (*Continued*)

Icon	*Uses and Meanings*
Summative Assessment or Grading 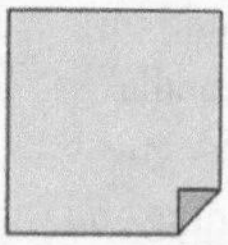	The sticky note icon represents summative assessments and grading. In ungraded or nonacademic settings, this icon could represent completion of required activities.

Using the Visual Vocabulary to Create Maps

First, let's look at the practical steps. Download the icons that represent the taxonomy of collaboration from the book resources website (https://vision2lead.com/learning-to-collaborate). The map diagrams in this book were created in Visio, part of Microsoft Office, but any drawing program will work. You simply need software that will allow you to insert graphics and rearrange them. You and your students will also need to be able to export the file as a single image.

In a program like Visio, begin with a blank page. You can use the " insert pictures" option to add in all the icons (Figure 7.1).

Next, sequence and arrange the icons to represent steps the group will take to complete the assignment (Figure 7.2).

Now, add in formative and summative assessments and any other notes (Figure 7.3). Notes can include numbers you can refer to in more detailed narrative descriptions as you can see in the examples provided throughout this book.

Alternatively, in a document program you can create a table and add the icons to each column (Figure 7.4). Add rows for the assessment icons and other notes.

These maps show an ordered collaborative process with a course sequence of lessons or units in mind. However, some may apply the collaborative principles in projects that are less linear than a traditional academic course. The map in Figure 7.5 was generated by a nonprofit organization to describe a collaborative project that included various types of activities that occurred simultaneously, with ongoing discussion at the heart of it.

You can also incorporate the icons into other kinds of representations, including mind or concept maps, graphic reporting, or sketch notes.

Figure 7.6 is an example with the icons placed in a mind map. Figure 7.7 shows icons (assessments) on a project map.

Relationships between the activities can also be illustrated and notes added (see Figure 7.7). As described previously, these approaches can be used in instructor-driven projects in which all students are following the same approach or a more flexible project in which students take the initiative to create their own maps. Use the icons creatively to represent the style and focus of your own projects.

Figure 7.1. Creating a map with Visio, step 1.

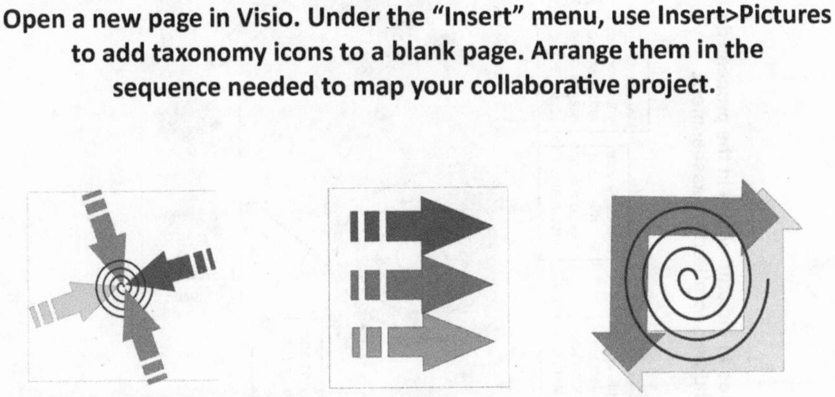
Open a new page in Visio. Under the "Insert" menu, use Insert>Pictures to add taxonomy icons to a blank page. Arrange them in the sequence needed to map your collaborative project.

Figure 7.2. Creating a map with Visio, step 2.

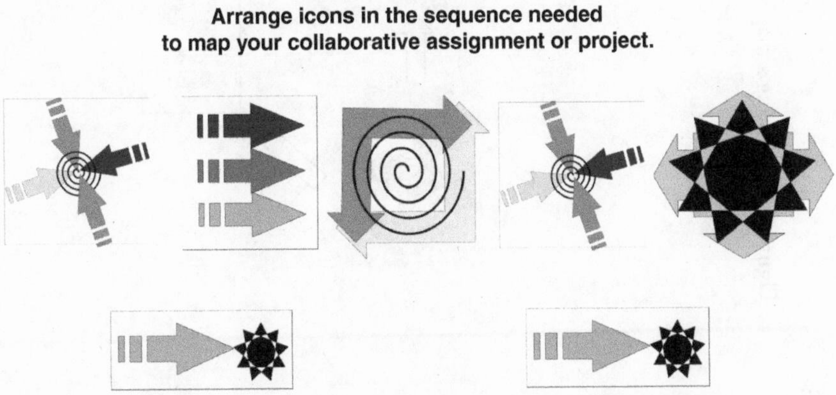
Arrange icons in the sequence needed to map your collaborative assignment or project.

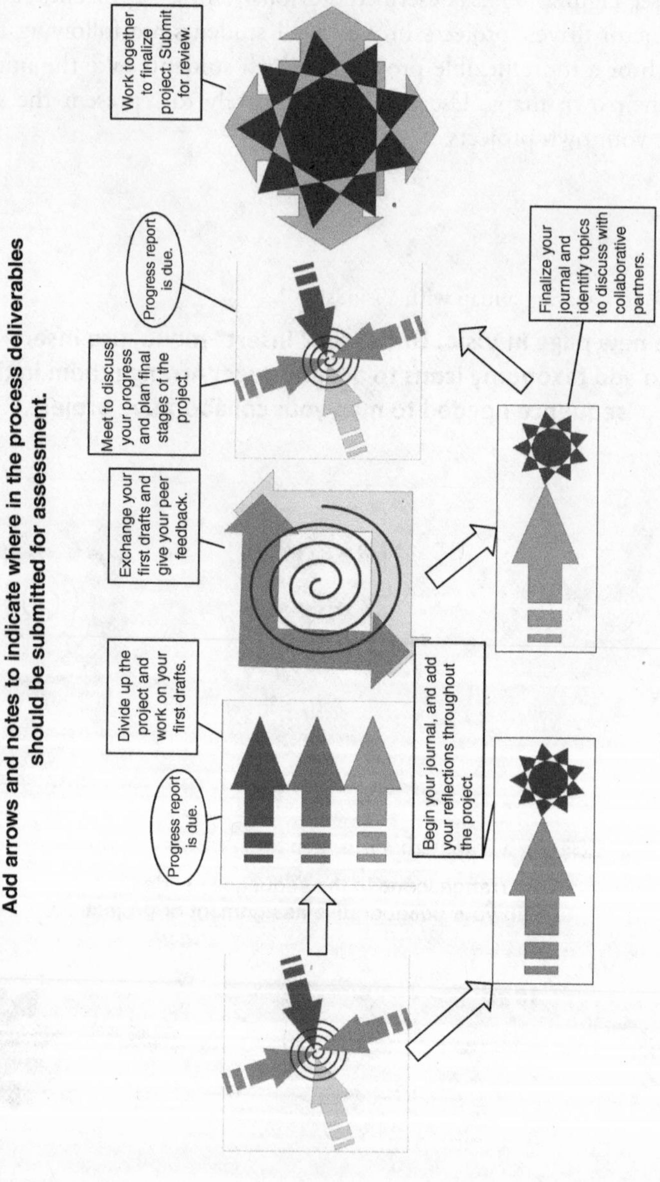
Add arrows and notes to indicate where in the process deliverables should be submitted for assessment.
Progress report is due.
Divide up the project and work on your first drafts.
Begin your journal, and add your reflections throughout the project.
Exchange your first drafts and give your peer feedback.
Meet to discuss your progress and plan final stages of the project.
Progress report is due.
Finalize your journal and identify topics to discuss with collaborative partners.
Work together to finalize project. Submit for review.

Figure 7.3. Creating a map with Visio, step 3.

Figure 7.4. Creating a map with a Word table.

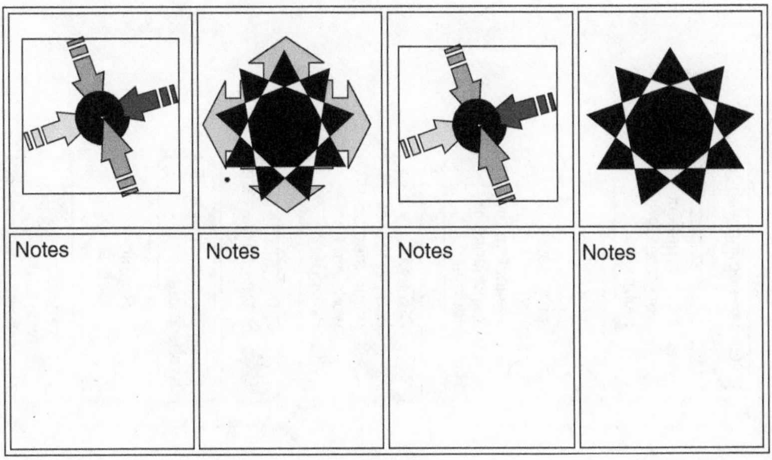

Figure 7.5. Creating a nonlinear map.

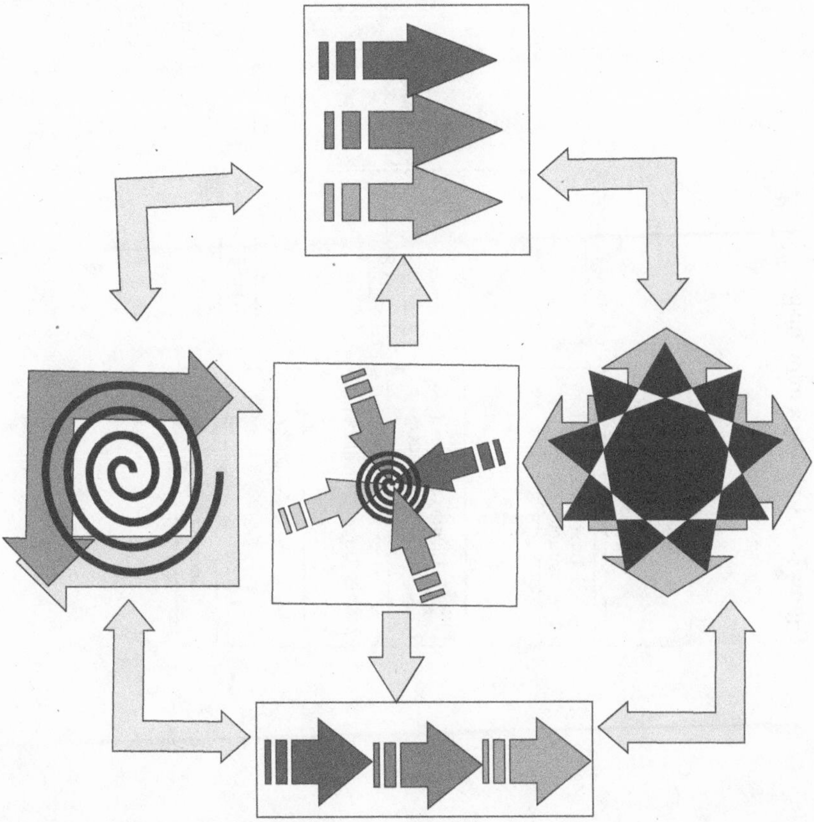

Figure 7.6. Creating a mind map.

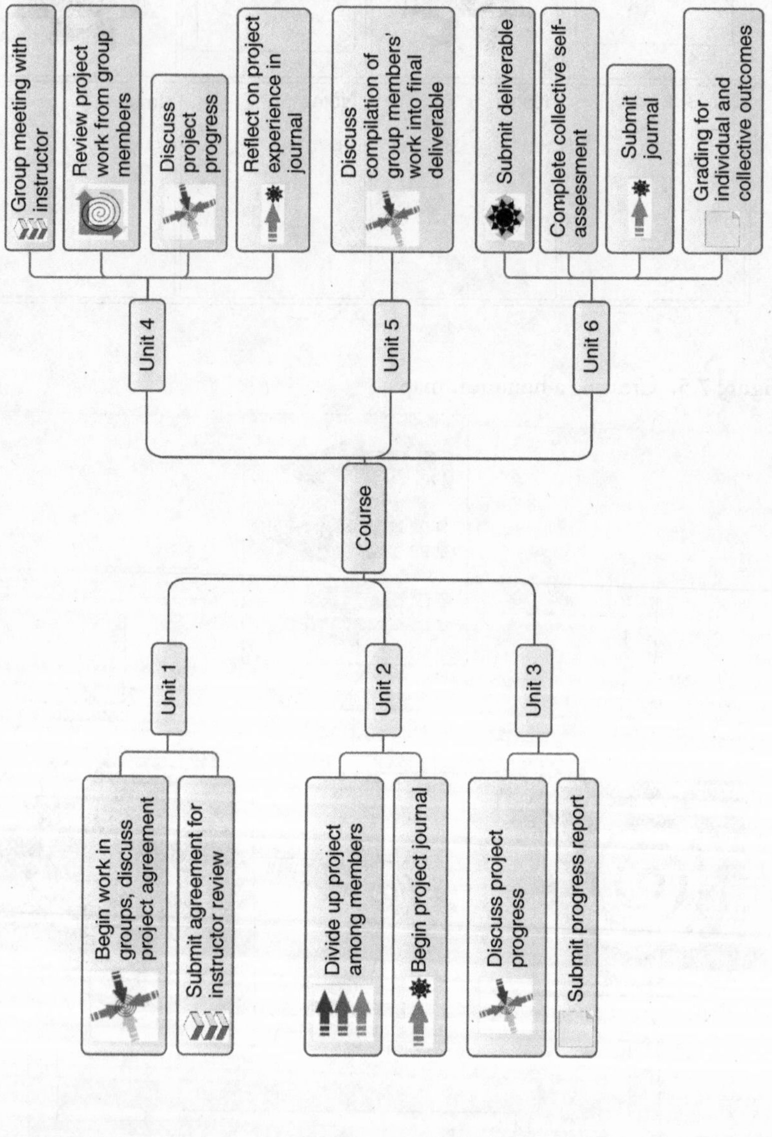

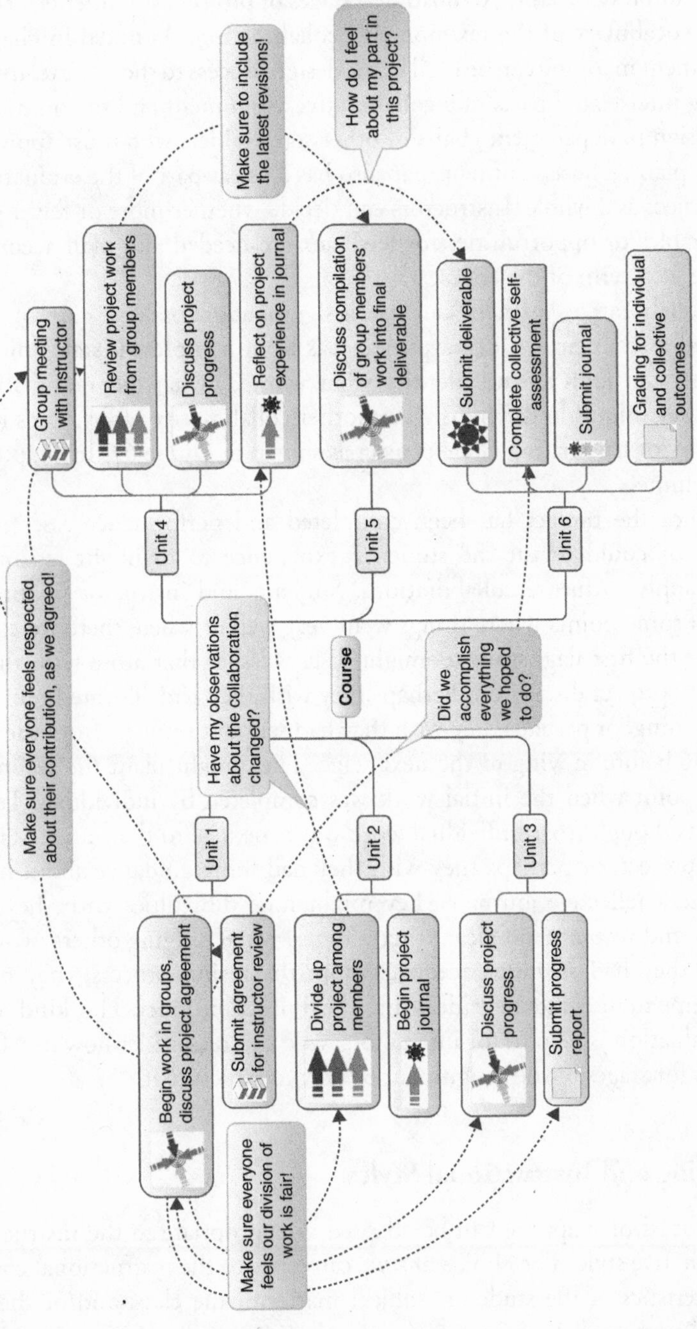

Figure 7.7. Showing relationships or reminders on a project map.

Mapping Assessments

The examples in chapter 6 illustrated stages of project assignments, using the visual vocabulary of the taxonomy of collaboration. As noted in chapter 5, assignment mapping can be used in the design process to show the relationship among interrelated parts of a collaborative assignment and to communicate the design to department chairs or other stakeholders who must approve the course plans. The assignment map also has a use as part of the evaluation for the project as a whole. Instructors can decide whether more or fewer graded deliverables or opportunities for feedback are needed and plan accordingly for the next term of the course.

Collaborative partners can use assignment maps as a part of collective self-assessments. Once a project has been completed, stakeholders or students can look at and identify what worked, what did not work, and what they might do differently in another collaborative effort. Let's look at the map for the writing circle project as shown in Figure 6.2 in chapter 6 of this volume.

Once the project has been completed and performance assessed, the instructor could revisit the students' experience to highlight lessons that could apply to future collaborations. Students and instructor might make note of some points where things went very well or where there were obstacles. At the first flag, students might discuss issues that arose with the preliminary project discussion. Perhaps they wish they had allocated more time for planning, or perhaps they wish they had sent out minutes from the initial meeting before moving to the next stage. They might plant the second flag at the point when the initial work was completed by individuals. Perhaps students thought that individual work was beneficial to their understanding of the project, or perhaps they wish they had more guidance about how to organize a reflective journal. They might note difficulties with the review process and recommend clear criteria to use when judging others' work. Or maybe they had so much feedback from the review process, they needed more time to integrate new ideas into the finished product. This kind of project evaluation is helpful for instructors, who can reconsider how much time to allot for stages of the assignment or how to structure it.

Mapping and Instructional Styles

The process of mapping can be adapted as appropriate to the instructional or facilitative style. The choice of style can relate to the instructional context, characteristics of the students, subject matter of the class, and/or the time allotted to the collaborative activity (Figure 7.8; see also chapter 5).

If students are inexperienced, there is a reason for consistency across all the groups in the class, or there is little time available for the collaborative activity, an instructor-driven style is appropriate (see Figure 7.9). In this case, the instructor can create a map for the assignment and provide it to each group. In a physical classroom the map can be displayed on the wall. This map could become a reference point for discussions throughout the project. Activities could include having each group make comments or indicate progress on the class map, perhaps using sticky notes that can be

Figure 7.8. Mapping and instructional styles.

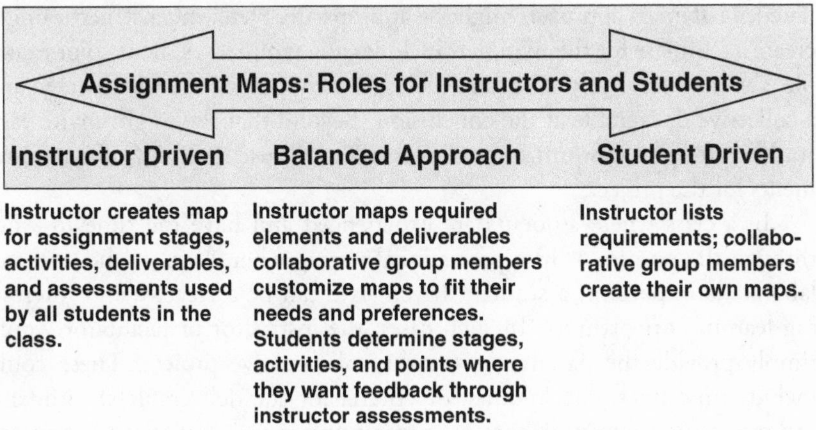

Assignment Maps: Roles for Instructors and Students
Instructor Driven
Balanced Approach
Student Driven
Instructor creates map for assignment stages, activities, deliverables, and assessments used by all students in the class.
Instructor maps required elements and deliverables collaborative group members customize maps to fit their needs and preferences. Students determine stages, activities, and points where they want feedback through instructor assessments.
Instructor lists requirements; collaborative group members create their own maps.

Figure 7.9. Instructor-driven style: Map with assessments.

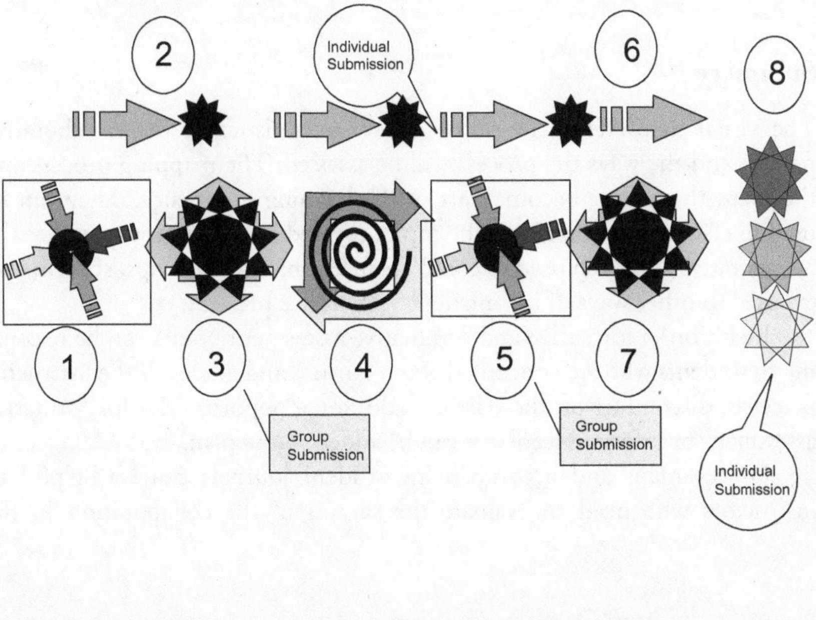

moved as the project progresses. Give each group a different colored marker or sticky notes. As the project unfolds, an image will evolve that represents the collective work of the entire class. Groups can add their own notes to the map, but all groups in the class are following the same general sequence and type of activity. In an online class using an instructor-driven approach, the map could be posted in the learning management system or in a class wiki. Collaborative software could also be used to create comments and progress notes as the projects progress.

In a class where students are prepared to take on the steps needed to determine what collaborative process will be used and how it will be coordinated, a balanced approach might be appropriate. Here, the instructor might create a template for the map that includes any required elements. For example, the instructor might require dialogue activities for the initial stage and a collective deliverable at the conclusion. Beyond that she might invite each student group to customize the process they will use to achieve the requirements for the project.

In a class where students are experienced and have the time to work through the process or in a professional setting where learning how to collaborate is important, a student-driven style can be a creative and interesting learning opportunity. In such cases, the instructor or facilitator would simply provide the parameters for the collaborative project. These could include time lines, checkpoints, or criteria for the deliverable(s). Students can create their own collaborative process and map it out. Each group can share their map with the class as the basis for discussion and learning about the kinds of ways different groups can approach the same problem.

Summary

The visual maps represent stages and characteristics of the collaborative process and the ways the process will be assessed. The mapping process and the maps themselves become part of the learning experience. They can be used to elicit discussion about the topics covered in the project as well as the collaborative approach used to complete it. By sharing the maps, students are exposed to other ways of organizing collaborative projects.

Inclusion of formative and summative assessment points can be reassuring to students who are concerned about fairness and grades. If the instructor perceives discomfort on these issues, additional opportunities for formative assessment or informal feedback can be added to the plan.

Project maps and accompanying student journals can be helpful to instructors who need to evaluate the success of the collaboration in the context of student competencies and achievement of course objectives. They can be used to troubleshoot problem areas and as the basis for course revision. For example, by comparing the maps and notes of multiple groups within the same course, the instructor may realize that students need more direction or more opportunities for autonomous work.

Key Questions: Prompts for Discussion or Reflection

- What is your typical instructional style? How does your style influence the ways you communicate with students to explain assignments? How does your style influence how you communicate expectations for assessment and grading?
- How could you use the visual communication strategies described in this chapter? What new strategies could you devise that would encourage students to embrace collaborative learning?
- Are your students ready to exercise leadership and decision-making with student-driven approaches? If not, how can you help them develop confidence and skills needed to learn how to collaborate?
- Will you need to change your instructional style to teach or facilitate collaborative learning experiences? If so, how will you learn these skills?
- How would you describe the factors that enhance or obstruct collaboration in your instructional setting? Which factors can you influence, and what steps will you take?

REFERENCES

Alfred, M. V. (2009). Social capital theory: Implications for women's networking and learning. *New Directions for Adult & Continuing Education, 2009*(122), 3–12.

Anderson, L., Bloom, B. S., Krathwohl, D., & Airasian, P. (2000). *Taxonomy for learning, teaching, and assessing: A revision of Bloom's taxonomy of educational objectives* (2nd ed.). New York, NY: Allyn & Bacon.

Bandura, A. (1977). *Social learning theory.* New York, NY: General Learning Press.

Bandura, A. (1986). *Social foundations of thought an action.* Englewood Cliffs, NJ: Prentice Hall.

Bandura, A. (1997). *Self-efficacy: The exercise of control.* New York, NY: W. H. Freeman.

Bauer, M., & Williamson, D. (2004). Using evidence-centered design to align formative and summative assessments. *Technology, Instruction, Cognition and Learning, 1*(1), 45–59.

Bichard, S. M. (2005). Managing for creativity. In C. L. Cooper (Ed.), *Leadership and management in the 21st century: Business challenges of the future* (pp. 299–304). Oxford, UK: Oxford University Press.

Billings, L., & Fitzgerald, J. (2002). Dialogic discussion and the Paideia seminar. *American Educational Research Journal, 39*(4), 907–941.

Bloom, B., Engelhart, M., Furst, E., Hill, W., & Krathwohl, D. (1956). *Taxonomy of educational objectives: Book 1. Cognitive domain.* New York, NY: David McKay.

Bloom, B., Krathwohl, D., & Masia, B. (1964). *Taxonomy of educational objectives: Handbook I. Affective domain.* New York, NY: David McKay.

Brookfield, S. D., & Preskill, S. (2005). *Discussion: Tools and techniques for democratic classrooms* (2nd ed.). San Francisco, CA: Jossey Bass.

Brown, H. G., Scott Poole, M., & Rodgers, T. L. (2004). Interpersonal traits, complementarity, and trust in virtual collaboration. *Journal of Management Information Systems, 20*(4), 115–137.

Bruner, J. (1966). *Toward a theory of instruction* (2nd ed.). New York, NY: W. W. Norton.

Bruner, J. (1971). *The relevance of education.* New York, NY: W. W. Norton.

Bruner, J. (1977). *The process of education* (2nd ed.). Cambridge, MA: Harvard University Press.

Bruner, J. (1986). *Actual minds, possible worlds.* Cambridge, MA: Harvard University Press.

Bruner, J. (1990). Culture and human development: A new look. *Human Development. 33,* 344–355.

Bruner, J., & Kearsley, G. (2004). Constructivist theory. Retrieved from http://tip.psychology.org/bruner.html

Cattaneo, K. H. (2017). Telling active learning pedagogies apart: From theory to practice. *Journal of New Approaches in Educational Research, 6*(2), 144–152.

Charan, R. (2001). Conquering a culture of indecision. *Harvard Business Review*, Reprint R0104D.

Cheng, X., Nolan, T., & Macaulay, L. (2013). Don't give up the community: A viewpoint of trust development in online collaboration. *Information Technology & People, 26*(3), 298–318.

Clarke, A., Fries, C., & Washburn, R. S. (2018). *Situational analysis: Grounded theory after the postmodern turn* (2nd ed.). Thousand Oaks, CA: SAGE.

Dalgarno, B. (2001). Interpretations of constructivism and consequences for Computer Assisted Learning. *British Journal of Educational Technology, 32*(2), 183–194.

DeVries, R. (1997). Piaget's social theory. *Educational Researcher, 26*(2), 4–17.

Dewey, J. (1916). *Democracy and education.* New York, NY: Macmillan.

Dewey, J. (1938). *Experience and education.* New York, NY: Macmillan.

Dillenbourg, P., Baker, M., Blaye, A., & O'Malley, C. (1996). The evolution of research on collaborative learning. In E. Spada & P. Reiman (Eds.), *Learning in humans and machine: Towards an interdisciplinary learning science* (pp. 189–211). Oxford, UK: Elsevier.

Dillenbourg, P., Baker, M., Blaye, A., & O'Malley, C. (1999). What do you mean by "collaborative-learning"? In P. Dillenbourg (Ed.), *Collaborative-learning: Cognitive and computational approaches* (pp. 1–20). Oxford, UK: Elsevier.

Dillenbourg, P., & Schneider, D. (1995). *Collaborative learning and the Internet.* Retrieved from http://tecfa.unige.ch/tecfa/research/CMC/colla/iccai95_1.html

Drucker, P. (2006). *The effective executive.* New York, NY: Harper Business.

Ford, R. C., Piccolo, R. F., & Ford, L. R. (2017). Strategies for building effective virtual teams: Trust is key. *Business Horizons, 60*, 25–34.

Gardner, H. (1983). *Frames of mind: The theory of multiple intelligences.* New York, NY: Basic Books.

Garrison, D. (2006). Online collaboration principles. *Journal of Asynchronous Learning Networks, 10*(1), 25–34.

Garrison, D. R. (2017). *E-learning in the 21st century: A community of inquiry framework for research and practice* (3rd ed.). New York, NY: Routledge.

Garrison, D. R., Anderson, T., & Archer, W. (2010). The first decade of the community of inquiry framework: A retrospective. *The Internet and Higher Education, 13*(1), 5–9.

Gilbert, S. W. (1992). Systematic questioning: Taxonomies that develop critical thinking skills. *Science Teacher, 59*(9), 41–46.

Gillies, R. M. (2017, Aug. 24). Promoting academically productive student dialogue during collaborative learning. *International Journal of Educational Research.* Retrieved from https://www.sciencedirect.com/science/article/pii/S0883035517300502

Glasersfeld, E. V. (1996). Footnotes to "The many faces of constructivism." *Educational Researcher, 25*(6), 19.

Gronlund, N. E. (2003). *Writing instructional objectives for teaching and assessment* (7th ed.). New York, NY: Pearson Education.

Hahapiet, J. (2008). The role of social capital in inter-organizational relationships. In S. Cropper, M. Ebers, C. Huxham, & P. S. Ring (Eds.), *The Oxford handbook of inter-organizational relations* (pp. 580–606). Oxford, UK: Oxford University Press.

Handy, C. (1995). Trust and the virtual organization. *Harvard Business Review, 73*(3), 40–50.

Hansen, M. T. (2009). *Collaboration: How leaders avoid the traps, create unity, and reap big results*. Boston, MA: Harvard Business Press.

Hansen, M. T., & Nohria, N. (2004). How to build collaborative advantage. *MIT Sloan Management Review, 46*(1), 22–30.

Hardy, C., Lawrence, T. B., & Grant, D. (2005). Discourse and collaboration: The role of conversations and collective identity. *Academy of Management Review, 30*(1), 58–77.

Hennessy, S., & Murphy, P. (1999). The potential for collaborative problem solving in design and technology. *International Journal of Technology and Design Education, 9*, 1–36.

Hibbert, P., & Huxham, C. (2005). A little about the mystery: Process learning as collaboration evolves. *European Management Review, 2*(1), 59–69

Hibbert, P., & Huxham, C. (2010). The carriage of tradition: Knowledge and its past in network contexts. *Management Learning, 42*(1), 7–24.

Huxham, C. (2003). Theorizing collaboration practice. *Public Management Review, 5*(3), 401–423.

Huxham, C., & Vangen, S. (2001). What makes practitioners tick? Understanding collaboration practice and practicing collaboration understanding. In J. Genefket & F. McDonald (Eds.), *Effective collaboration: Managing the obstacles* (pp. 1–12). New York, NY: Palgrave.

Huxham, C., & Vangen, S. (2004). Realizing the advantage or succumbing to inertia? *Organizational Dynamics, 33*(2), 190–201.

Huxham, C., & Vangen, S. (2005). *Managing to collaborate: The theory and practice of collaborative advantage*. Oxford, UK: Routledge.

Johnson, D. W., & Johnson, R. T. (Eds.). (1996). *Cooperation and the use of technology*. New York, NY: Simon & Schuster.

Kenis, P., & Oerlemans, L. (2008). Social network perspective: Understanding the structure of cooperation. In S. Cropper, M. Ebers, C. Huxham, & P. S. Ring (Eds.), *The Oxford handbook of inter-organizational relations* (pp. 289–312). Oxford, UK: Oxford University Press.

Kouzes, J. M., & Posner, B. Z. (2017). *The leadership challenge* (2nd ed.). San Francisco, CA: Jossey Bass.

Krathwohl, D. (2002). A revision of Bloom's taxonomy: An overview. *Theory into Practice, 41*(4), 212–218.

Krathwohl, D., Bloom, B., & Masia, B. B. (1964). *Taxonomy of educational objectives: The classification of educational goals. Handbook II: Affective domain.* New York, NY: David McKay.

Levesque, V. R., Calhoun, A. J. K., Bell, K. P., & Johnson, T. R. (2017). Turning contention into collaboration: Engaging power, trust, and learning in collaborative networks. *Society & Natural Resources, 30*(2), 245–260.

Loewenstein, J., & Mueller, J. (2016). Implicit theories of creative ideas: How culture guides creativity assessments. *Academy of Management Discoveries, 2*(4), 320–348.

London, S. (2005). Thinking together: The power of deliberative dialogue. In R. J. Kingston (Ed.), *Public thought and foreign policy.* Dayton, OH: Kettering Foundation Press.

Lotia, N., & Hardy, C. (2008). Critical perspectives on collaboration. In S. Cropper, M. Ebers, C. Huxham, & P. S. Ring (Eds.), *The Oxford handbook of inter-organizational relations* (pp. 366–389). Oxford, UK: Oxford University Press.

Maraon, N., Benarroch, A., & Gaomez, E. J. (2000). What is the relationship between social constructivism and Piagetian constructivism? An analysis of the characteristics of the ideas within both theories. *International Journal of Science Education, 22*(3), 225–238.

McInnerey, J. M., & Roberts, T. S. (2004). Collaborative or cooperative learning? In T. S. Roberts (Ed.), *Online collaborative learning: Theory and practice* (pp. 203–215). Hershey, PA: Information Science Publishing.

Miyake, N. (1986). Cognitive interaction and the iterative process of understanding. *Cognitive Science, 10,* 151–177.

Morrison, G. R., Ross, S. M., & Kemp, J. E. (2004). *Designing effective instruction.* Hoboken, NJ: John Wiley/Jossey Bass Education.

Moshman, D. (1997). Pluralist rational constructivism. *Issues in Education, 3*(2), 229.

Moshman, D., & Geil, M. (1998). Collaborative reasoning: Evidence for collective rationality. *Thinking and Reasoning, 32*(2), 2001.

Novak, J. D., & Gowin, D. B. (1984). *Learning how to learn.* Cambridge, UK: Cambridge University Press.

Oakley, B., Felder, R., Brent, R., & Elhajj, I. (2004). Turning student groups into effective teams. *Journal of Student Centered Learning, 2*(1), 9–34.

Obayashi, S., Inagaki, Y., & Takikawa, H. (2016). The condition for generous trust. *PLoS Biology, 11*(11), e0166437.

Palincsar, A. S., & Brown, A. L. (1984). Reciprocal teaching of comprehension-fostering and comprehension-monitoring activities. *Cognition and Instruction, 1*(2), 117–175.

Palincsar, A. S., & Herrenkohl, L. R. (2002). Designing collaborative learning contexts. *Theory Into Practice,* 41(1), 26–32.

Phillips, N., & Hardy, C. (2002). What is discourse analysis? In *Discourse analysis* (pp. 2–18). Thousand Oaks, CA: SAGE.

Piaget, J. (1952). *Origins of intelligence in children.* New York, NY: International Universities Press.

Piaget, J. (1971). *Biology and knowledge.* Edinburgh, UK: Edinburgh Press.

Prawat, R. (1993). The value of ideas: Problems versus possibilities in learning. *Educational Researcher, 22*(August), 5–16.

Reid, H. L. (1998, August 10). *The educational value of Plato's early Socratic dialogues.* Paper presented at the Twentieth World Congress of Philosophy, Boston, MA.

Rodriguez, A. J., & Berryman, C. (2002). Using sociotransformative constructivism to teach for understanding in diverse classrooms: A beginning teacher's journey. *American Educational Research Journal, 39*(4), 1017–1045.

Rourke, L., Garrison, R., Anderson, T., & Archer, W. (2000). *Assessing teaching presence in a computer conference environment.* Retrieved from http://communitiesofinquiry.com/sub/index.html

Salmons, J. (2016). *Doing qualitative research online*. London, UK: SAGE.

Schwab, J. (1983). The practical 4: Something for curriculum professors to do. *Curriculum Inquiry, 13*(3), 240–265.

Simonin, B. L. (2003). The importance of collaborative know-how: An empirical test of the learning organization. *Academy of Management Journal, 40*(5), 1150–1174.

Soanes, C., & Stevenson, A. (Eds.). (2004). *Concise Oxford English Dictionary* (11th ed.). Oxford, UK: Oxford University Press.

Sorensen, E. K., Takle, E. S., & Moser, H. M. (2006). Knowledge-building quality in online communities of practice: focusing on learning dialogue. *Studies in Continuing Education, 28*(3), 241–257.

Talja, S., Tuominen, K., & Savolainen, R. (2004). "Isms" in information science: Constructivism, collectivism and constructionism. *Journal of Documentation, 61*(1), 79–101.

Teaseley, S. D., & Roschelle, J. (1995). The construction of shared knowledge in collaborative problem solving. In C. O'Malley (Ed.), *Computer-supported collaborative learning* (pp. 69–97). Heidelberg, DE: Springer-Verlag.

Toffler, A. (1970). *Future shock.* New York, NY: Random House.

Vangen, S., & Huxham, C. (2003). Enacting leadership for collaborative advantage: Dilemmas of ideology and pragmatism in the activities of partnership managers. *British Journal of Management, 14,* S61–S76.

Vangen, S., & Huxham, C. (2012). The tangled web: Unraveling the principle of common goals in collaborations. *Journal of Public Administration Research and Theory, 22*(4), 731–760.

Vygotsky, L. (1978). *Mind and society: The development of higher mental processes.* Cambridge, MA: Harvard University Press.

Vygotsky, L. (Ed.) (1987). *Thinking and speech: The collected work of L. S. Vygotsky.* New York, NY: Plenum.

Vygotsky, L. & Kozulin, A. (1986). Thought and language.

Wasserman, S., & Faust, K. (1994). *Social network analysis: Methods and applications.* Cambridge, UK: Cambridge University Press.

Windschitl, M. (2002). Framing constructivism in practice as the negotiation of dilemmas: An analysis of the conceptual, pedagogical, cultural, and political challenges facing teachers. *Review of Educational Research, 72*(2), 131–175.

Wood, D., Bruner, J., & Ross, G. (1976). The role of tutoring in problem solving. *Journal of Child Psychology and Psychiatry, 17,* 89–90.

Yazici, H. J. (2004). Student perceptions of collaborative learning in operations management classes. *Journal of Education for Business, 80*(2), 110–118.

Zhu, W., Newman, A., Miao, Q., & Hooke, A. (2013). Revisiting the mediating role of trust in transformational leadership effects: Do different types of trust make a difference? *The Leadership Quarterly, 24*, 94–105.

Zozakiewicz, C., & Rodriguez, A. J. (2007). Using sociotransformative constructivism to teach for understanding in diverse classrooms: A beginning teacher's journey. *Educational Policy, 21*(May), 397–425.

ABOUT THE AUTHOR

Janet Salmons is an independent scholar, a writer, and a coach through Vision2Lead. She wrote *Doing Qualitative Research Online* (SAGE Publications, 2016) and *Qualitative Online Interviews* (SAGE Publications, 2015) and edited the *Cases in Online Interview Research* (SAGE Publications, 2012). Forthcoming books include *Find the Theory in Your Research*, *Getting Data Online*, *Publishing from your Doctoral Research* with Helen Kara, and *Collaborate to Succeed in Higher Education and Beyond* with Narelle Lemon. She coedited *A Handbook of Research on Electronic Collaboration and Organizational Synergy* (IGI Global, 2009) with Lynn Wilson. Salmons is the methods guru and lead writer for SAGE's blog community, methodspace.com, and a reviewer for the SAGE Research Cases. She received The Mike Keedy Award (2018) from the Textbook and Academic Authors Association, given in recognition of enduring service to authors.

Salmons served as a dissertation supervisor and qualitative methodologist for the Walden University PhD program in educational technology from 2016 to 2017. She served on the doctoral faculty of the Capella University School of Business from 1999 to 2016, and she was honored with the Harold Abel Distinguished Faculty Award for 2011 to 2012 and the Steven Shank Recognition for Teaching in 2012, 2013, 2014, 2015, and 2016.

Salmons received a BS in adult and community education from Cornell University, an MA in social policy studies from Empire State College (State University of New York), and a PhD in interdisciplinary studies and educational leadership at the Union Institute & University. She lives and works in Boulder, Colorado.

INDEX

step-by-step directions for flipping your course, along with plenty of examples, answers to typical questions, and variations for hybrid and online courses."—***Linda B. Nilson**, Director Emeritus, Office of Teaching Effectiveness and Innovation, Clemson University*

This book is for anyone seeking ways to get students to better learn the content of their course, take more responsibility for their work, become more self-regulated as learners, work harder and smarter during class time, and engage positively with course material. As a teaching method, flipped learning becomes demonstrably more powerful when adopted across departments. It is an idea that offers the promise of transforming teaching in higher education.

Stylus

22883 Quicksilver Drive
Sterling, VA 20166-2019

Subscribe to our e-mail alerts: www.Styluspub.com

Also available from Stylus

The Blended Course Design Workbook

A Practical Guide

Kathryn E. Linder

"Katie Linder has written a practical, smart, and even compassionate book on blended course design. Drawing on both research and experience, she walks readers through the process of creating blended courses that will challenge and engage students, providing plenty of examples and tips along the way. This is the essential guide we need to ensure our students will be successful in blended courses." —***Peter Felten***, *Assistant Provost for Teaching & Learning, Elon University*

The Blended Course Design Workbook meets the need for a user-friendly resource that provides faculty members and administrators with instructions, activities, tools, templates, and deadlines to guide them through the process of revising their traditional face-to-face course into a blended format. The book will help each instructor who uses the text to develop a unique course by making choices about his or her course design based on student learning needs for their chosen topic and discipline.

Flipped Learning

A Guide for Higher Education Faculty

Robert Talbert

Foreword by Jon Bergmann

"Think you know what flipped learning is? Think again. I had to. It's not about technology, recording your lectures, or physical classrooms. This is why you have to read Robert Talbert's *Flipped Learning*. It's the definitive book on the pedagogy, with a new and refreshing perspective. Talbert relates flipped learning to theories of motivation, cognitive load, and self-regulated learning and gives

(Continued on preceding page)